A POOR MAN'S PROOF
FOR THE EXISTENCE OF GOD

D1383236

John N. Constantino

PAULIST PRESS
New York/Mahwah, N.J.

100% of the royalties from this book will be used to support the needs of disadvantaged children in America's inner cities.

Bible quotes were obtained from *The Jerusalem Bible,* Copyright 1966, Doubleday & Company, Inc. The use of the first person pronoun and the names of the main characters in the story are fictional.

Library of Congress Cataloging in Publication Data

Constantino, John N., 1962–
    A poor man's proof for the existence of God / John N. Constantino.
      p. cm.
    ISBN 0-8091-3262-1 (pbk.)
    1. God—Proof. I. Title.
BT102.C66   1991
212'.1—dc20   91-25349
                                                 CIP

Published by Paulist Press
997 Macarthur Blvd.
Mahwah, New Jersey 07430

Printed and Bound in the United States of America.

Contents

Acknowledgements

An inadequate word of thanks

to God, for everything

to my Mom and Dad, who taught me to seek God from the time I was very small

to my brother, Paul, who opened my eyes to the power of brotherhood

to the monks of the Saint Louis Abbey, who showed me who God was

to the English professors at Cornell University who taught me how to write

to my close friends, who taught me how to laugh, and to understand that no man is an island

to the patients whose faith inspired the writing of this book

and to my wife, Michele, who taught me what it means to love.

To Michele and Anna

And to my Godchildren, Oliver and Bonnie Marie

Introduction

I do not believe in God—that's correct, I do not
"believe" in God.
Rather, I *know* there is a God.
—*excerpt from a letter of a grieving father to his dying son*

I am told that in a reflective moment after an address
to a large crowd of his people, Gandhi was questioned
about his stance on Christianity, and much to the surprise
of those who were interviewing him, he replied, "If Chris-
tians were Christian, I'd be a Christian." True enough, if
everyone followed the dictates of his or her own religious
beliefs in everything they did, the world would have a lot
fewer problems. Nearly all world religions uphold similar
principles of charity, self-discipline and consideration of
others. Why is it, then, that there is so much selfishness
and abandonment of these principles in day-to-day lives,
even by people who claim to subscribe to religious belief?
Some might say that this is explainable on the basis of
human weakness and an inherent tendency in all of us
toward selfishness and thoughtlessness. Some would say
that the range of "evil-doing" in our world (from occa-
sional transgressor to hardened criminal) represents simply a spectrum of human weakness and self-centeredness
from very mild to very severe.

In this book I have chosen to look at it a different way.

1

I have considered the "root of evil" not to be a reflection of a person's "bad-"ness, but of their lack of *motivation* to do good. Thus, although our responses to religious teachings are affected to some degree by "what kind of people we are," I believe that the more important determinant of that response is how motivated we are to respond. And that, in turn, depends entirely on just how seriously we take God. It is my feeling that most of the time, when people's actions represent a departure from their own religious beliefs, it is a matter not so much of hypocrisy, but of difficulty in maintaining a meaningful belief in the elusive notion of a spiritual God. Once that faith is eroded, it is easy to put God on a shelf, as it were, and act as if he were not a real part of the picture. And it can be very difficult to believe in God firmly, and live by that belief, when so many other distractions, desires, and tangible influences dominate our everyday life.

Thus perhaps if the notion of God could be clarified, if God were easier to believe in, and faith were more solid and alive, religious beliefs would be acted upon with more regularity. The implications of making a decision about whether or not to truly *live* by our religious beliefs can be profound. Devotion to God in any religion carries with it a commitment and a responsibility to love and care for all members of the human family, as well as a heartfelt desire to seek God and his work in all things. It makes sense that in dealing with a God who is all-powerful and who loves each person infinitely, the degree of a believer's devotion would be not only wholehearted but *constant* in everything he or she does. On the other hand, if the decision is made *not* to firmly believe in God, one is really only bound by an instinctual "conscience" or a system of values or ethics that governs his or her freedom to do whatever is pleasing in life. Though few of us limit ourselves to such a system, it is conceivable that non-belief in God could justify a life of selfishness or hedonism.

What's interesting is that for some reason, most of us

lie somewhere in between those two extremes of devotion and non-devotion, at least in terms of what our actions demonstrate. The reason it's interesting is that this implies that most of us fall somewhere in between believing in God and not really believing in God, or not really taking God seriously. I suppose it's possible to believe in God and not take him seriously, but that, to me, is as unreasonable as being out in a boat and not taking a hurricane seriously. If the kind of God that most world religions talk about is real, he must be worth our undivided attention—to be alive without being close to him must be no better than being dead. I think that's serious. Each of us, therefore, ought to decide whether we think God is real or not. If he is real, he is as real as the book that is in your hands and as real as your hands themselves. That is what being real is all about. He may not be visible as those things are, but he is no less real. On the other hand, if God is not real then he is simply not real. For some reason, though, most of us insist on adopting a stand in between these two extremes—and thus between devotion and non-devotion, between belief and non-belief. Does that make sense? Can you "kind of" believe in God? Can you "kind of" believe in the Atlantic Ocean? Is there such a thing as being "kind of" pregnant?

Belief in the existence of God is very difficult and very controversial. But if indeed the degree of our belief dictates our response to religious teaching, then it is very important. The degree or "quality" of belief in God is, in turn, very much dependent upon why it is that we believe or disbelieve in his existence. If religious belief is only a tradition that is handed down from one generation to another, then "belief in God" will not be taken more seriously than any other tradition. If one believes in God because there is no other suitable explanation for the creation of the world, then God is a creator but no more than a creator. He can be put on the shelf as a creator who vanished after the creation was accomplished and may not even be alive anymore. If one is unsure of the existence of God, he

3

or she may decide to put some limited amount of effort into religious activity just in case God is real, to avoid eternal punishment in an afterlife. If one is skeptical of God's existence, he or she may find it foolish to spend a lot of time thinking about God.

Faith should be an all or nothing thing. You either believe in God or you don't. The problem is that it is very difficult to make a good decision about that, so most of us bounce around some. Many do not make their final decision, ironically enough, until they are about to die, which is like deciding on a starting line-up for an athletic team during the last minute of the last game of the season. That's better than not deciding at all, and granted, it takes a long time to make good decisions sometimes; but to take too long can defeat the purpose of making the decision in the first place. God either exists or he doesn't. He either lives among us or not. You have to get that down first before you go any further with religion. That is what this book is all about.

This is a story of three very different people who are struggling with the question of whether or not to believe in God. It is written not only for people who are unsure of whether or not God exists, but for believers and nonbelievers alike. It is concerned both with reasons to believe in God and with reasons NOT to believe in God. It criticizes invalid assumptions that are commonly used to support or refute the existence of God. In somewhat of a stepwise fashion, it attempts to lead the reader to real evidence in support of the notion that God lives, and in the process it offers an original modern-day proof for the existence of God. It deals with the nature of God, with the essence of spirituality, and with the quintessential manifestation of that spirituality in our day-to-day lives, which is human love. It shows in considerable detail how love transcends the capabilities of our biological brains and thus constitutes evidence for the existence of a spiritual aspect of our humanity. It shows how that spiritual aspect of our humanity is the medium through which we experience God. And it deals with the profound implications that the existence of a living God should have on the way that we conduct our lives.

In essence, true belief in God depends heavily on asking very important questions. Sometimes the answers to those questions are difficult to accept. Sometimes we even hesitate to ask the questions for fear of what the answers will be. Although this book is devoted to arriving at answers, I believe that life is not so much a matter of getting answers as it is of asking the right questions. As you read on, regardless of whether or not you agree with how the questions in this book are answered, I hope that the mere asking is as rewarding to you as it has been to me.

ONE

The Questions

Dear Father Hesburgh:
They've got me down. Flat on my back . . . with plaster,
sand bags and hot water bottles. . . . Whenever my cancer acts up—and it is certainly "acting up" now, I turn
inward a bit. Less do I think of my hospitals around
the world, or of 94 doctors, fund raising and the like.
More do I think of one divine Doctor, and my own
personal fund of grace. Is it enough. . . . How do people endure anything on earth if they cannot have God?
                              —*from a letter written by*
                    Dr. Thomas Dooley, December 2, 1960

Religion . . . is the opiate of the masses.

                                          —*Karl Marx*

About a year ago I was sitting in a cafeteria in New
York City having lunch by myself, and a friend of mine
from work, a middle-aged man who had recently come to
the United States from Israel, happened to walk into the
same place and joined me. I remember that he was particularly concerned about some atrocious event that had just
happened in one of the public schools, which had made
headlines in all of the newspapers that day. So we got to
talking about how kids grow up in the city, and the kinds of
things they get exposed to, and for some reason, somewhere in the conversation, I asked him whether or not he

thought it was important for kids to believe in God while they were growing up. He looked at me, sat back in his chair, shook his head and smiled. "You shouldn't ask me such a question." I felt bad for putting him on the spot with a sensitive topic. Before I could change the subject, he continued, "You see, *I* beleef, John," he said in his usual broken English, "that there is no such thing as God. Two of my uncles died in a concentration camp at Auschwitz. To me, that is where God died, too, if ever there *was* God before that." He paused for a moment and added, "No God could stand by and watch what has happened in this world and not stop it." And that was the end of the conversation about God. Even though I thought I believed in God, I had nothing to say to counter his argument. I knew that my reasons for believing couldn't hold a candle to his reasons for *not* believing.

I went home that night thinking about poor people. I mean really poor people. Because in the back of my mind I couldn't stop wondering how any of those poor victims of Auschwitz could keep believing in God while they were waiting to be exterminated. The more I thought about it, the more it made me think that there were a lot of good reasons *not* to believe in God. And it made me wonder, too, if any of my reasons *for* believing in God were any good. I had grown up in a religious family, so almost out of habit I still went to church pretty regularly. I had questioned my faith deeply in college, and was almost talked out of it altogether, but I never arrived at any real *answers* either for or against my religious beliefs. So I retained a sort of "hope" in God, which satisfied my "need" for a higher being at times when the limitations of my humanity got the best of me, but which otherwise didn't profoundly affect the way I conducted my life. Having had that faith rattled by what my friend had said, I went to church that Sunday inwardly wondering whether or not I really believed in God.

The church that I went to on Sundays was a beautiful

stone building with high arched ceilings and brick floors and simple wooden benches. It had been built and cared for by English monks who, for generations had also taught at my old high school, which was across the street. Like the monks themselves, the church was completely devoid of decoration. The altar in the center of the church was an enormous granite block. There were a few small altars on the periphery of the church, each with an impressionistic stone statue or a bronze crucifix. And there were lit candles everywhere. It was always dark and musty inside (the black robes of the monks faithfully harbored that same musty smell) but it was not offensive in any way—rather, it was inviting; the darkness and mustiness enveloped you, and in the austerity of the surroundings, tried to lift you away from what was earthly or material, to search for anything that might exist beyond what you could physically see around you. It tempted you—almost *dared* you in a gentle kind of way—to hand yourself over to God.

But where was he? As I looked around I remembered many other times, especially when I was in high school, when I would come to this same place to find him and reassure myself of his existence. Often, when I felt my faith wavering, I would walk inside and kneel in front of one of the crosses on the side altars and pray for God to come to me or help me, or let me get to know him better. But he never came, not once. I never heard his voice. Perhaps I didn't listen enough, but in a way I was afraid to listen because I didn't want to be disappointed if I didn't hear anything. I never knew if he was there.

The monks of that church, on the other hand, were so completely convinced that God was there, that in taking their vows, they promised to stay at that single church and monastery for life, to worship God there. The church was their home. Sometimes they'd be in there meditating in silence, sometimes they would chant prayers together for hours, and then other times you'd even see one of them in a T-shirt and blue jeans mowing the lawn or barbecuing for dinner. They were an odd mix of personalities, the monks, but in all honesty, they were some of the happiest people I had ever known. And I know I wasn't the only one who thought that—almost everybody who knew them flocked to them in one way or another, in search of the profound secret of their happiness. Their peace was unshakeable. Even though I had known them since my boyhood, the secret of their peace and happiness had surely eluded me.

One of the things that had always fascinated me about the monks was how they accepted living a life of poverty. And they were poor by choice. Not as poor as the people of Auschwitz, and certainly not persecuted that way, but they otherwise made themselves pretty poor. They didn't even own the clothes they wore. Were they punishing them-selves for something? Or was that a part of the secret of their happiness? I asked one of them one time when I was in twelfth grade why he decided to be a monk if he knew he was going to have to be so poor.

"I made up my mind to be a monk," I remember him explaining, "when I fell in love with God. The first time I met him, he was only there for a split second, and then he was gone, because I couldn't keep my concentration on him. My mind was too easily distracted, my heart was clut-tered with other things. Material things, money, cars, clothes, schedules. . . . And I realized that unless I got rid of all those other distractions, I'd never be able to hang onto him. Because when other desires fill your heart, God vanishes. And I knew that I wanted in the worst way to be with him all the time. So what we do here is get rid of the material things because they're just distractions. We take only what we need."

"But did you have to become a monk to do all that?" I asked him.

"When I first came here and told them I wanted to be a monk," he said, "they put me in a black robe and told me I couldn't talk to anybody for six months. To tell you the truth, after two weeks, I started losing my mind, so I went to the abbot and told him that I wanted to quit because the silence wasn't getting me any closer to God, and I asked him if he had any other suggestions. Do you know what he told me? He looked at me and said, 'Go sit in your cell, and your cell will teach you everything.' And I did, and it did—he was right. . . . Does that answer your question?" I told him it did, and thanked him, and decided never to ask religious people personal questions again. I never knew exactly what he meant by what he said, but I gathered that there was something about being poor that made it easier for him to see God. And his relationship with God was certainly what made him happy.

There was only one other person that I knew of who had the same kind of happiness that the monks had, and he, too, happened to be poor. He was a gas station attendant at the corner filling station three blocks from the house where I grew up. I didn't know him well enough to know whether or not he believed in God, but I have a feeling he did because you could often hear him mumbling, "Lord have mercy," particularly when he was helping an overly demanding customer. Whenever I was in the car with my mom or dad and they needed gas, they would drive into that gas station, and there he would be, at the car window before you could roll it down, asking what he could do for you. There was no smile in the world like this man's smile. He wore one of those old leather airplane pilot hats with the ear flaps up, and an oil-smeared jump suit that God only knows what color it was when it was new, and he was a little overweight. But he had more energy than any ten people I had ever known. He was completely devoted to what he was doing, and his business wasn't cars, it was people. He'd always ask the customers what kind of a day they were having, and people knew that he really cared, and some of them would literally tell him right through their car windows what was going on in their lives.

And everybody knew it wouldn't go any further than the gas pump because he wasn't a gossipping kind of person. He just cared, and he loved what he did. Everyone knew that whether you opened up to him or not—even if you didn't say a word to him—after the hood got slammed down and the gas cap got tightened, he would always have something nice to say to you; you would always drive out of there knowing that your day had just been made a little bit richer for having seen him. You knew that in his *heart* he wanted you to have a good day. He didn't even own the gas station, he had just worked there for years. People had offered him all kinds of "better" jobs but he graciously turned them all down. No surprise, since that literally was his station in life. It was his office, his pulpit, his inner sanctum. Like the monks, he had the secret to a kind of fulfillment and happiness that I had always sought, but never found. I thought of him as I walked down the aisle of the church that Sunday, and there was an emptiness inside of me; I was facing the prospect of losing my faith altogether, and losing with it my chance of life after death, even some of my reasons to live, and perhaps my only means of obtaining a very rare and wonderful kind of happiness in this life.

As I looked for a seat I was bumped by a little old bag lady, half out of her mind, shuffling down the aisle for a pew close to the front, repeatedly making the sign of the cross and mumbling to herself. I sat down next to a lady with a black fur coat whose perfume was so strong that my nose wouldn't let any air in, so I had to breathe through my mouth. I recognized a lot of business faces in the church that day. My boss was there—he had just given us a talk that week about how sales were down, and if we didn't start spending more of our leisure time (nights and week-ends) entertaining and catering to customers, we were going to be replaced. Four pews down was a man whom I had seen twice earlier in the week at two different bars with two different secretaries; now he was with his wife and family.

I stopped looking around and tried to tune into God, but not much happened. As I listened to the sermon I tried to extract from it any smattering of reinforcement for my faith that it could offer, but nothing really helped very much. After the sermon, when it came time for the collection basket to go around, the priest announced that all of the money collected would be sent to missionaries in South America to help feed the people there. The woman in the fur coat next to me nodded piously and reached into her purse. The diamond on her ring finger was so large that it almost prevented her hand from advancing into the depth of her pocketbook. Perhaps that was her excuse. All she could manage to pull out was a crisp one dollar bill, smiled at the man carrying the basket and dropped it in. I looked at her for about fifteen seconds in complete disgust at how cheap she was, but she didn't even notice. I decided I had had enough of church so I got up and left. In retrospect, before getting so disgusted, I should have realized that I had given one less dollar than the lady with the diamond, but I didn't think about that at the time.

About two weeks later I went to visit a friend who was in the city hospital dying of lung cancer. His name was Sonny Joseph. He was a 46-year-old high school science teacher and football coach who was the last person in the world you would expect to get lung cancer—he had never smoked a cigarette in his life. He had taught me and coached me in high school, and I had kept in pretty close touch with him ever since that time. He was the one that all of the kids in the school looked up to and that everybody could talk to, and he was the one that you went to when you had a problem—long before you subjected yourself to the school counselor. He had been diagnosed with cancer about six months prior to my visit, and in that period of time the doctors had done for him all that they could do. He was supposed to die within the next two-to-four weeks. The cancer had spread everywhere—his bones, his liver, his brain.

When I first walked into his room, I couldn't help but notice how terrible he looked. His body was a physical wreck, although mentally he seemed as sharp as ever, at least at first. His left eye was stuck—"looking" over to the left, as if out of the single window of his barren private hospital room. Actually (I later found out) he was almost completely blind in that eye—the reason it was stuck was apparently that one of the small metastatic tumors in his brain had destroyed the roots of the nerves to that eye. His other eye moved fine, and if you looked at it by itself, it seemed as sharp and deep and blue as ever—but without the company of the other eye, when you looked at them both together it left the pathetic initial impression that this once robust and intelligent man was losing his mind as well as his body.

He was in good spirits, and we talked for a while about his family and people that we both knew, and then we got to talking about how he was feeling about everything that was happening to him, and finally I asked him if he was scared. "No," he answered, "I'm not that scared. I think I'm gonna make it. I've got God with me and nothing is impossible with God. He'll get me out of the mess I'm in— he'll rescue this body and make it alive again. Just wait and see." At first I thought he was talking about dying and going to heaven but as he continued, it became clear that he literally thought God would somehow heal him. He finally came out and said it, "Somehow I know in my heart that it's not my time to die. God's gonna get me through this cancer."

I was shocked. Frankly, I thought he was nuts. We all knew what the doctors had said about his cancer. It made me angry to think that nobody had spent the necessary time with him to help him accept the fact that he was going to die. I could see where his family would encourage him to think positively, and they were hoping against hope that he was right. But somebody (maybe more removed from his immediate family) should have sat down with him and laid it all out for him. So it occurred to me that maybe I should take it upon myself (since I knew him pretty well) to

14

help him to realize what was happening. I had no idea what I was getting myself into. He was sure that God would save him. Everyone else—including his doctors, his family, and me—was sure that he was going to die, and I felt like he deserved to be prepared to die. I just wanted him to be at peace, and to be as ready as he could be. "Sonny, lots of people get cancer, and I know God doesn't want you or any of them to suffer. But maybe he's getting ready for you to be with him." I didn't know what else to say.

Sonny was *not* one of these people who, for the first time in their life, desperately cling to God when they find out they are about to die. He was never afraid of death. Or anything, really. He had walked with God his whole life. He went to church every day, gave what he could to the poor, and dedicated his life to his teaching and his family. Somehow he felt that God just wasn't yet ready for him. He felt like he knew God pretty well and he felt that he would somehow "know" when God was ready for him, but the time hadn't come quite yet. So after we talked about it for a while, he sensed my disbelief about the whole thing, and he finally looked at me and said, "You don't believe God *can* save me, do you?"

"I don't know," I replied. I was at a loss for words. I didn't want to take away his hope, but I wanted him to realize he was about to die. I waited for him to say something.

"You believe in God, don't you?" he asked me.

"Sure," I replied, trying to hide my uncertainty.

"Then how could you *not* believe that he could cure this cancer? God can do everything."

"I guess he could if he wanted to," I answered. "Otherwise he wouldn't be God." I was at a loss for anything more profound to say than that. In my heart, I wasn't sure what I believed about God. "Not that he wouldn't *want* to cure you, Sonny . . . but things just don't work out that way."

"That's just a nice way of saying that you really don't

believe he *can* cure me! You're looking at me as if I've got corn flakes in my brain or something. Well, by God, there are *tumor* flakes in my brain, the doctors told me so, but that doesn't mean I've lost my mind! Sure, my eye doesn't work any more and sometimes I forget to get up and pee when I have to, and they tie me down sometimes at night because they say I get delirious, even though I never remember it. . . ." He almost began to cry, but managed to hold back any tears. "I'm fighting this thing so hard," he said. "It gets the best of me sometimes. But let me tell you something. There's more to me than just the brain and flesh that this cancer is rotting its way through. I have a soul that no cancer can ever take away. And that's the part of me that's talking to you right now. My soul belongs to God and it's keeping me alive."

"Anyway," he continued," I'm thinking straight now, and who knows, maybe it'll be the last day I'll ever be able to think straight, and maybe it won't. I want you to think straight with me because maybe we won't ever have the chance to do this again." He stared down at the foot of his bed, then looked up and whispered, "Listen to yourself. . . . Think about what you've been saying. . . . The way you're talking there's no way you could believe in God, but I can't believe that you mean it. *Do you believe in God?* If you do, you know that he can save my life." As he looked at me quietly, he searched my blank stare as if to uncover the secrets of my soul. I had no idea what to tell him. There was something almost terrifying about being there, so desperate was this man in the circumstance of an impending death, yet so consumed in the fire of his faith—you could see it in his eyes, that fire, and it was something that made me very uncomfortable. I had seen this kind of hope in dying people before, and had come to regard it as a fantasy that was generated out of desperation. But it was so obviously alive in this man. Could it be real? Or was he just insane? Either way, what business was it of his whether I believed or not? If I were to tell him something he didn't

16

want to hear, would it just make him more upset? I didn't know what to say.

"I do believe in him," I finally said. "I just don't think he involves himself too much in what happens in this world."

"That's garbage," he sharply replied. "If you think that God doesn't interact with this world, how can you say that you believe in him? There wouldn't be anything to believe *in*. It would be impossible for you to know anything about him."

"Everybody has different opinions about God, Sonny. I'm entitled to mine and you're entitled to yours."

"Opinion nothing. There's only one truth, son. God either is or he isn't. No matter how many opinions are out there circulating about him, there's only one truth. When you believe in God, there's no opinion about it. Only truth. If you don't think that what you believe in is the truth, then you don't believe in anything." He paused for a moment. "I'm not talking about some theory. I'm talking about God, a real God who's almighty like God's supposed to be—a God whom *it means something* to believe in."

"I'm not sure if I know who that God is," I said. "I've never seen him myself. He's never interacted with me. And for someone who has so much power, he lets a hell of a lot of bad things happen in this world."

"That he does. But let's face it, most of the bad things that happen in this world are things that we do to one another. Don't blame God. He gave us the ability to control ourselves and take care of one another. It's not his fault if we don't use it."

"Maybe you're right," I said. "But he still makes himself pretty scarce in this world."

"Would it make a difference to you if he were sitting at the foot of this bed in the *flesh*? Would that help you to believe in him?"

"Sure it would," I answered.

"Then you've proved to yourself that you don't believe in God. If you believed in him, it wouldn't make any difference whether he appeared in the flesh or not. He would be just as real whether you could see him or not. So God's invisible . . . does that mean he's less real because you can't see him with your eyes? He either is or he isn't. You either believe in him or you don't. If he's real—visible or not—he's as real as your hands and this bed are real. If you believed in him, it wouldn't matter to you that you can't see him."

He had a point. One thing I was realizing very quickly was that he was indeed, at least for the time being, as sharp as ever, despite what the tumor was doing to his brain. He was making me think about things I had never even thought about before. "I guess I never thought about him as being real like these kinds of things are real," I confessed.

"Then you never believed in God. That's all there is to it. If you believed in God like he was something real, you wouldn't be talking like this." He stopped for a moment and looked around the room. "Put your hand on this bed rail," he said suddenly. "Go ahead, put your hand on it. Touch it. Is it real to you?"

"Sure it's real, Sonny," I answered.

"If God is not every bit as real to you as this bed rail, then you don't believe in God. That's all there is to it. He may be invisible, but that doesn't mean he's any less real." He had a very intense look on his face; he was trying with all his heart to get through to me. "I mean, imagine if God was standing right here in the flesh, listening to you talking about whether or not he was real. First you say you believe in God, then you say he might not be real. Wouldn't you feel strange telling him that to his face? Let me tell you something, he *is* here, just as if he was in the flesh. He's always with you everywhere. If you believed in him, you'd know that about him. And you probably wouldn't talk about him the way you do. Your whole life would change if you really believed he was with you."

"Maybe it would," I answered, and I thought about

18

what I would be doing if God were with me every minute. "Actually I have a lot of doubts about him."

"That's OK. Everybody does sometimes. But just remember one thing: just because you're in between believing and not believing doesn't mean that God is somewhere between being real and not being real. You're the one who has to get your mind straight. Not God."

"You're trying to convince me that I don't believe in God."

"That's always the first step in finding him. You have to be able to admit that you haven't found him. I'm telling you that you don't believe in God. And you probably don't NOT believe in God. You've never made up your mind either way. You haven't done what it takes to come up with an answer, so you just ride the fence," he said.

"But how can anybody reach a conclusion about God? You can't prove his existence with science. He's invisible, you can't hear him or feel him or touch him. There's no *evidence* you can collect about him. You can't take a picture of him. So how can you ever be sure about whether God is or he isn't. There's nothing to go on one way or the other."

"There *is* evidence for God," he replied, "good evidence. But since God (for the most part) is *spiritual* in nature, a lot of that evidence is spiritual, too. That's not to say history and psychology and philosophy and science aren't important in proving God—I think most of them are very necessary. But those disciplines aren't equipped to deal directly with what God is made of, so they can only get you so far. They deal with information that our senses can gather and that our brains can put together, and that's all very important, but to prove God, you have to go one step beyond that. You have to confront God as the spiritual being that he is. And the only way we have of gathering any knowledge about things that are spiritual (and invisible and untouchable) is to use that part of ourselves that's spiritual in nature—our own "souls"—that's the part of our humanity that allows us to interact with God."

19

"So you're saying that to prove God's existence you have to somehow "interact" with him. Is that right?"

"Sure," he answered. "I mean, how do you know that your hand exists?"

"Well, obviously," I said, "I can see it and touch it. . . ."

"Exactly. It's the same way with God. The evidence is ultimately in the experience. It may take other kinds of evidence first to make that experience meaningful or even possible. But it's the *experience* of God that turns theory into reality. Just like it's the experience of trees and rocks that makes you believe in the reality of trees and rocks."

"So what would I have to do to experience God?"

He didn't answer me at first. "What makes you think I have an answer to that?" he replied, after a long moment of silence.

"You seem to have a lot of answers," I said half-sarcastically.

"Not this time," he said, and smiled. He smiled in a way that made it look to me like he *did* have an answer, but that he was going to make me come up with it myself. My punishment, perhaps for being sarcastic with him. But I had no answers either, so I didn't say anything. He shook his head sadly. "All I can do is help you prepare yourself," he said. "But in the end, you're the one who has to experience God for yourself. Only then will he be real to you."

"What do you mean by 'preparing' myself," I asked him.

"Like I said, first you have to examine all of the 'material' evidence you can get your hands on from philosophy and history and science to help your brain decide whether or not God is a real possibility. Then, at the same time, you have to start getting in touch with your own spirituality, because that's the only part of you that's capable of truly experiencing God."

"So what if I don't get in touch with my own spirituality?" I wasn't even sure whether or not I believed in any such thing as spirituality.

"If you want to badly enough, believe me, you will. I'll help you. But for now, I'll answer your question with a question: if you were sitting in a pitch dark room, how would you know whether or not there was a picture of a tree painted on the wall?"

"There'd be no way to tell unless you turned on a light," I replied.

"So, in just the same way that light is necessary for us to visually experience material objects, spirituality is the medium through which we experience God. That spiritual experience of God is what faith is really all about. It's not just blind belief, it's spiritual evidence. *Faith is the evidence of things unseen.* To come to a conclusion about the existence of God, you're going to have to use a better part of yourself than just your eyes or your senses or your brain, because God isn't visible or touchable in that way. You have to find inside of yourself the best part of what you are—a part of yourself that's just like God—which is the only part of you that can sense and experience the presence of God. When you've found that, and you've gathered enough evidence to satisfy your brain that God is a real possibility, then all you'll have to do is listen and he'll touch you and you'll know beyond a shadow of a doubt that it's him. That's what true faith is all about."

I was trying to make sense of how he was trying to put the whole thing together, but I had so many questions about the individual elements of this "overview" of faith— the "evidence," the concept of spirituality, the "finding" of God—that I didn't know where to begin.

"One thing I could never understand," I said to him, "is that if faith is so powerful and God is so powerful, why can't he find a way to make it easier for us to see him? You're telling me about all these things I need to do to prepare myself to see God, and none of them are that easy. The evidence is hard to find, Sonny, and spirituality is a difficult concept to hang your hat on. Why should it be so hard? If God were really around, don't you think he'd

21

make it *easier* for us to believe in him? You would think he'd *want* us to believe in him and he's gotta know how hard it is to have faith in him. Just the fact that it's so difficult has to make you wonder if he's really there."

"So what do you want, a miracle?" he asked me.

"That wouldn't be bad for starters," I said. "Let's put it this way: if he cures you, I'll believe in him. But he's not going to cure you and I don't even want to think about it or hope for it because that's not fair to you. It's not going to happen, Sonny."

"Even if I was cured, that would be a dumb reason to believe in God," he said.

"Why?" I was surprised to hear him say that.

"Because then for the rest of your life, your belief in God would depend on just that one miracle. Every time you started to doubt him you'd say, '*wait a minute—I can't doubt God; because remember that one miracle I saw?—that's proof that there must be God.*' And it would all stop right there for you. You'd never even try to find out anything else about him. He'd already be in your hip pocket."

"So what's so bad about that?"

"What's so bad about that?" he echoed. "I'll tell you what's so bad about that. It means that God's just a magician. And God's not just a magician. You're missing the whole point if you spend your life thinking about him that way. Magicians take physical objects and do unexplainable things with them. The best part of God isn't what he can do with physical things. He's spiritual. If you don't understand him on a spiritual level, not only have you thrown away the greatest part of God, you've thrown away the greatest part of yourself. Because you have to use your own spirituality—your *soul*—to find God the way he really is. If you just believe in God because you've seen your miracle, you don't have to use your soul. If you don't use your soul, you never experience God as the spiritual being that he is. It's as simple as that." He stopped for a minute and shook his head. "It's so sad how people get carried away with the physical aspects of God. Millions of people hang their faith on things like shrouds and visions and arks. Maybe those are things that God gives us every once in a while, but that's not what God is all about."

"But to *know*," I persisted, "that he could really make the impossible happen. . . ."

"So *what*," he interjected, "if he can make the impossible happen? So what if he can take a rock and make water come out of it? So what if he can make fireballs in the sky, or cure the incurable or make the oceans split apart? So what if he can take material things, things that you can touch and see and hear, and do strange things with them? Is that the important thing about God? Or is the important thing that he cries when we cry. He holds us when our bodies fall apart. He feels pain when we suffer because he loves us more than he loves himself. He loves us *infinitely*. You can't comprehend that. If we were really able to feel all of his love—and we can't because we let ourselves get so ravelled up in the *things* this stupid world confuses us with—but if we could really feel it, it would probably rip our hearts right out of our chests."

"So maybe it's better we can't feel it."

"Are you kidding me? You'd give anything to feel it if you understood what it was. When we die, that's what heaven will be—to be able to be loved by God and feel every bit of it. That's all that matters after you die. That's all that matters *before* you die if you're smart enough to realize it. And everybody who's got a heart can make themselves smart enough to know that the love of God is what it's all about." He stopped and looked down at his body, with all of its sores and bruises—a pathetic shadow of what it was when he coached me football—and it almost got the best of him to look at himself that way, but he took a deep breath in and sighed and then looked up and smiled.

"The important thing about him," he continued, "isn't what he does to material things, but how he's made of something better than anything that you can see or hear or feel. He's spiritual. Isn't that what God is all about? And he's given you that same spirituality so that you can be immortal, too, and self-aware, and capable of love that doesn't have any end—you're not just some material, biological *thing*. That spirituality of yours is all you need to experience him and understand him. When you ask him for magic tricks to convince you that he's real, you just throw all that away. You're telling God that you don't want to understand him that way—that you refuse to believe in him that way." He paused and said, "Do you think God wants us to understand him like that? It's no wonder he keeps the miracles away. That way, we'll be forced to use our own spiritualty—the best part of our humanity—to find him and understand the truth of who he really is. Miracles are petty things that get people very confused about what God is."

"That's a pretty big excuse to make for God."

"It's not an excuse," he replied. "Look at it another way. It's like understanding how your parents love you. . . . Do your parents love you?"

"Of course my parents love me," I answered him. "You know my parents." (He had known my parents pretty well during the time I was in high school). "What does that have to do with anything?"

"How do you know they love you?"

"I don't know, they put their whole lives into raising my brothers and sisters and me. What are you getting at?"

"Suppose that your parents, with all the best intentions, had spoiled you rotten. So that the only time you recognized that they loved you was when they gave you something. Something tangible. If your understanding of their love depended so heavily on those material things, would you really know how much they loved you? I don't think so."

"But being spoiled rotten and asking for one miracle are hardly the same thing."

"They're exactly the same if you're going to allow your

belief in God to depend on that one miracle. Your faith in God has to come from what he makes you *feel,* not what he makes you see. You have to hear him with your heart. If you don't understand him that way, you're like a spoiled kid that waits for his parents to bring him another present before he acknowledges their love. You've got to experience him as he really is. God speaks to you in whispers. He's spiritual. You have to use your own spirit to find him. You have to hear him with your heart."

"Frankly, Sonny," I said to him, "I wish he'd speak up a little."

TWO

The Nature of God

God is spirit, and those who worship must worship in spirit and truth.
                                              —*John 4:24*

Dear God:
I believe in you without any doubts at all. I like the way you are invisible so that we have to make up our own minds about you. Good idea.
                              Love, Bo (age 10 yr.)
—*Excerpt from DEAR GOD: WHAT RELIGION WERE THE DINOSAURS?, David Heller*

He was really harping on this concept of the *spiritual nature of God* which I wasn't sure that I understood very well. I wasn't sure that I believed in the existence of anything spiritual. Was there really something that existed outside of the physical world that was yet a part of this world, and as real as material things were real? I had always wondered whether or not there was a part of myself—a soul—that existed outside of the atoms and molecules and cells that my body was made of. If I had been convinced that there *was* such a thing as spirituality, perhaps it would have been easier for me to believe in a spiritual God. But that wasn't the case at the time. If nothing else, I needed some kind of assurance that spirituality was real before I could go any further in following Sonny's line of reasoning about God.

26

I went to visit him again a few days later, but he didn't look well at all, although he never let on that he was feeling poorly. I was going to let him rest but he urged me to stay, and he wanted to know how I was feeling about the conversation we had had before. So we started talking about it and by the time a few minutes had passed, we were right back to where we had left off.

"How am I supposed to know," I asked him, "that part of myself is spiritual? What does that even mean?"

"Have you ever loved anybody?" he asked me.

"Sure I have, but that doesn't mean I'm spiritual," I said.

"You don't think love is spiritual? You can't see it or touch it or hear or smell or taste it. But it's *real*. If it's not spiritual, what is it?"

"It's probably just like our thoughts and our other emotions," I answered. "Something that our brain does to make us feel a certain way. A special nerve cell in one place connects to another nerve cell in another place and they're linked to whatever part of the brain is responsible for emotions, and when they get turned on, you feel something. What's so spiritual about that?"

"So you're saying that the things you think and feel are things that your brain is doing but not really what *you're* doing."

"What do you mean?" I asked him.

"You're saying that your brain is this thing in your body that makes you feel everything you feel. So in a sense there's really no 'you.' When 'you' feel something it's just an effect of different processes in your brain that make your brain pleasing or painful to itself. But there's no you. No agent of self-awareness or control over what your brain is doing. Just a brain and a body. No spirit. No person aside from the nuts and bolts of the body."

"Right, I mean, I *guess* that's what I'm saying."

"But you know that you can think and choose for yourself. If all you had was a brain, everything you did would be automatic. You'd be like a computer or a robot. Brains are just collections of nerve cells connected to one another. No matter how complicated the brain, biological cells are biological cells. All they can do is react to stimuli and transmit their reactions to one another. They can't spontaneously decide to initiate things. They can't be 'aware' of what they're doing. So even when you hook millions of them together—even in the most complicated patterns of circuitry—they're still just nerve cells. Like computers are just chips and wires. They may be able to store memories, they may be able to alter their connections in response to different stimuli, they may even be able to coordinate mechanisms for self preservation and social interaction. But that's all a biological brain can do. If all you had was a brain, you wouldn't have free will. You wouldn't be aware of yourself. You'd be automatic. Constantly responding in complicated ways to the things that were going on around you—but just responding. Is that really how you think it is? In your heart you have to know that there's more to you than just that."

"Maybe, maybe not," I answered. "Maybe we just THINK we have control over our thoughts. Maybe all of our thoughts (and even what we call our conscience) are programmed responses to things that are going on around us. You know yourself how some things *automatically* make you feel a certain way without even having to think about it. Maybe all the things we think about and feel are ultimately like that, even if we *feel* like we're somehow actively in control. Why *couldn't* they just be functions of chemical reactions in our brains? You don't have to think to make your heart beat. So maybe you don't have to "think" to be able to think. It just happens in response to things. When you hear X, you think Y. When A happens to you, B is the way you feel. It may not always be quite that simple—you said it yourself, the thoughts and feelings and interactions might get pretty complicated—but in the end they could

28

just be predictable responses to the information gathered by the nerves. It could all just be the result of the circuitry in our brains. Maybe there is no free will."

"But we don't always just react to things. What about when I want something that doesn't belong to me? If my brain just 'reacted', I'd take it. But I can fight the urge to do what my 'animal instincts' tell me to do." He paused for a moment. "I mean I can go along about what you're saying as far as animal instincts go, but not with my thoughts and my feelings. I'm human. I know I have free will."

"But how do you know that the will to fight the urge to steal isn't also somehow programmed into your subconscious brain? Maybe it was drilled into you from the values your parents taught you. When there are conflicting interests it can be difficult to exercise or express those values, but then your brain has to make a choice. . . ."

"*I* have to make a choice," he interrupted.

"Maybe, Sonny, it really is just your brain. To use your example of making the decision not to steal something, it *could* be that all your brain has to do is recall certain memories, access various impulses and desires, and then weigh them against each other according to their importance. Whichever way the scale tips, that dictates the decision that will be made and the behavior that will result. There may be memories of getting caught or punished for stealing in the past. Different people may have a stronger or weaker urge to steal. Guilt will enter into it, too, since people have subconscious ideas about right and wrong from what their parents taught them. I mean, psychologists have been proposing models for this from the time of Sigmund Freud— how the id, ego, and superego function and interact to determine what a person's behavior will be like. The bottom line is that these difficult choices you're talking about might not have anything to do with free will. They just might represent complicated explorations of the brain's own conscious and subconscious impulses. Which would mean that ultimately the outcome is always predictable. So it's possible that all of our behavior could be predetermined by the wiring in our brains."

It was obvious to me that the prospect of being "predetermined" was upsetting to Sonny—it was to me, too, when I really thought about it—but he listened quietly and open-mindedly, and you could tell by looking at him that the wheels of his mind were turning; I had the feeling that he had thought about all of these things many times before.

"You might say," I added, " 'At least I have the choice of whether to explore my own brain or not. If I want, I don't have to think about anything at all.' But it's easy to see how that, too, could be profoundly influenced (if not completely determined) by the balance of the millions of impulses and memories and ideas that have been ingrained into our brains through our experiences from the time we were born. Likewise, when we feel 'in control' of our behavior, it's possible that this is just our brain's way of producing a certain kind of pleasurable sensation in response to processes which are producing favorable behaviors, but which we can't begin to understand. And if all that's true, if 'we' are nothing more than the nuts and bolts and wiring (so to speak) of our neurologic circuitry, then what place is there for free will?"

"But everything we do isn't just a reaction," he replied. "You're human. You know what it's like to think a new thought. To have a new idea. To give of yourself for a cause. To create even a small work of art. To fall in love. Not just to decide between things or compare other things to yourself, but to *initiate* ideas and feelings and thoughts. Somewhere in the core of our humanity, there has to be something more than a brain, that makes us capable of that phenomenon of initiation and allows us to have the **free will** to direct our own destiny. To look *outside of ourselves* and then make choices that involve more than just our own instincts and impulses and circuitry." He paused for a moment. "I mean, I'm sure that a lot of the things we do are motivated exclusively by what's happening in our biological brains. And maybe there are some people who rely exclusively on their circuitry to make all of their decisions for them, as if they're on autopilot or something (whether voluntarily or involuntarily). But don't you think that at some level we all have the *capability* to rise above those brain forces that influence our behavior? If not, we wouldn't have any control over ourselves. We wouldn't be human. In fact, if you want to get technical about it, we would never even be 'at fault' for anything because if our brains were in control, there wouldn't be any way to avoid the consequences of its impulses. Is that really how you think it is?"

"Maybe so. You and I know plenty of people who probably shouldn't be blamed for how they act because they obviously don't have much control over what they do. A lot of people are violent or rude or selfish by habit— they grew up in it, they were taught to accept it, they practice it, and they never think twice about it. Why *wouldn't* you think it was programmed into their brains?— lots of times they don't seem to have any control over what they do at all. You can't blame them for something they don't have control over."

"I'm not *blaming* them. But I have more faith in their humanity than to say that they have no ability to control it. Sure, some people won't exercise their ability to control their instincts and live by what their heart tells them to do. But it doesn't mean they're incapable. It doesn't mean that they're predetermined."

"I know what you mean, Sonny, and I'd like to believe you. But just because we *feel* like we have free will doesn't necessarily mean we have it. The brain is a complicated thing. . . . so complicated that we may never really know what it does to make us feel or think the way we do."

"But it's no more than the sum of its parts. It's a neurologic machine, and you can't go ascribing all kinds of magical properties to it just because you can't completely understand it."

"Who's ascribing the magical properties?" I quickly replied. "You're the one who's talking about free will and spirituality."

"What I'm trying to tell you is that there are certain qualities of being human that you and I and every human being on earth are aware of, which can't be ascribed to brain function. And it's those qualities that are the essence of what we call our souls, the seat of human spirituality. And the nature of spirituality is such that it gives us the power to override the influence of our instincts and make decisions that rise above the stimulus-response mechanisms of our biological brains.

"Which kind of qualities are you talking about that can't be ascribed to brain function?"

"I think there are at least two. One I can *prove* is not attributable to brain function, the other is just my intuition. I'll start with the 'intuition one,' which is self-awareness. It's hard for me to believe that a neurological machine—that's what we would amount to if what you're saying is true— would try to 'understand itself' or even entertain the possibility of things that are so abstract as free will or spirituality. Maybe you think it's part of the machinery of the brain to generate fantasies about self-explanation. I think that's a little far-fetched. Think about it, of all the animals on this earth, human beings are probably the only ones who are truly self-aware. We know that we are *ourselves,* and we wonder where we came from and what will happen to us after we die. It's hard for me to believe that we're like that *just* because we have more complicated circuitry than the other animals. Just because you can build a bigger computer doesn't mean it can know and wonder about itself. So even though I can't prove it, I believe strongly that self-awareness is a quality that could only come from something beyond the brain.

"What's the other one?"

"The other is that we can love. The fact that we can love is proof to me that at least part of us is spiritual."

"How can you be so sure that love isn't just another function that's performed by our brains?" I asked him.

"Your brain doesn't love," he answered. "Love is different from the kinds of things a biological brain can do. No matter how you look at it, true love is never just a response to a stimulus."

"How can you be so sure about that?" I asked him. "Maybe our tendency to 'love' is just our brain's way of responding to that self-awareness that you're talking about; to the knowledge that we're alone in this cold world, and that we're going to die alone, so we'd better connect ourselves to whomever we can in this life, to give our life any meaning at all. Maybe love is just something that we do out of a deep-seated *fear* of being separated from the rest of humanity. So we use love to get close to other people, because our self-awareness makes us realize that we are each individual and alone."

"But love isn't like that," he said. "I'll grant you that love is a way of connecting ourselves to our fellow man, but if that was its only goal, it would ultimately be self-seeking; it would be saying, *'I want to be close to you because I'm terrified of being alone.' What makes love so different is that it puts the other person first before the self.* When you really love someone, you love them for *their* sake, not just yours. It can motivate you even to lay down your life for the person you love. If love were just a 'mechanism of connection' generated in response to the fear of separation, who would allow their own life to be extinguished for the cause of loving someone else? It's possible to love people who you may never even see again, or who may never *ever* love you in return. So it's more than just a means to the connection you're talking about. (And a connection made out of love is much different than a connection made out of fear). Love has a life of its own; it's something that exists *outside* of the domain of our self-preserving brains."

He was quiet for a moment. "To look at it another way," he continued, "biological things are predictable.

When Pavlov's dogs heard a bell, they salivated like crazy. The brain connects stimuli to responses—it can get very complicated—but in the final analysis, that's all it can do. Love doesn't work that way. It's an *unstimulated* response that we can initiate ourselves. It's *not* predetermined. It's something that issues forth from our souls and allows us to break away from the instincts that keep us centered on ourselves. Love doesn't even make rational sense. You can love others even when they hate you. It can motivate you to do what your brain or your rationality would never let you do. It can motivate you to die for someone you love. And the reason is that *love allows you to look outside of yourself.* All of the other things we call emotions and impulses and desires center around ourselves—how we feel, what we want, how to help ourselves survive and dominate our surroundings. But love is completely different. Love requires being in touch with someone other than yourself and considering what they need and want and desire. When we remove ourselves *from* ourselves in that way, not only do we see *ourselves* in a new light, but new options arise in our relationships with those we love. Our love gives us ideas and motivations of its own that can override the influences of our brain. And it's that ability to look beyond ourselves that gives us the option to act on more than just our own impulses. Only when we exercise that option do we become free from the dominance of our instincts. Only then can we have free will. Only then can we be fully human." There was a long silence.

"You're doing everything you can," I said, "to show me that there *is* something spiritual about myself, aren't you. I want to believe you. I know what it feels like to love somebody, and part of me is telling me that you're right." I was starting to understand him but I still wasn't sure what to think.

"Look at it another way," he said. "If love were just a part of our biological machinery, it never would have stood the test of evolution."

34

"Evolution?"

"That's right. Imagine if you were a creature who lived with the dinosaurs, and you were the first one to evolve the ability to love. All of the other creatures would take advantage of you. You would probably sacrifice yourself at some point so that your creature friends could survive: if food was scarce, you would be the one to starve; if there was danger, you would be the one to sacrifice yourself to protect the others. If love were just a biological trait, it would have died out a long time ago—evolution only spares the traits that make animals most fit to survive. But love is still a part of us, and with love you can do more than just survive."

He pulled a copy of the Bible out from under his bed, opened it to a marked page, and said to me, "Here, I'll read you something." He started reading a passage out of one of St. Paul's letters:

Love is *always* patient and kind; it is never jealous; love is never boastful or conceited; it is never rude or selfish; it does not take offence, and is not resentful. Love is always ready to excuse, to trust, to hope and to endure whatever comes. Love does not come to an end.

"This wouldn't get very far as a biological survival manual," he said as he closed the book. "Our biology tells us to survive, but love shows us how to do much better than that. We can choose to follow our animal instincts and survive, or we can choose to love and do more than just survive. If we couldn't love, we'd just be slaves to our instincts—but with love we can override the instincts of our animal brains. We can look beyond ourselves. We can think on our own. We can change. We can care. We can sacrifice. These, I think, are human capabilities that have to tell you that something outside of our brain is enabling us to override our instincts. That's what love is all about to me. It's the cornerstone of our free will."

This was something that had never crossed my mind before—that love was so fundamentally different from human "instincts," and that it might have something to do with what we called "free will." Was *love* the thing that made me human? Was it evidence that there existed a part of me that was spiritual like God was spiritual? In thinking about it before I had always lumped love together with my concept of other emotions and thought processes. But Sonny was right. Love was different. It didn't fit the kind of "patterned response" quality that other biological mechanisms fit. It wasn't predictable. It wasn't self-seeking or even self-preserving. It put the other person first.

From the time of early childhood when we first become aware of ourselves, we all long to love and be loved, and we're usually willing to do very irrational things for the sake of love. Real love doesn't expect or ask for anything in return. We often love people against our better judgment. So love seemed to be a force in and of itself, and not so much a matter of biological circuitry. It was different than just a brain reaction. It seemed to exist beyond what my neurons or my senses could generate on their own. And perhaps my ability to love was a product or a reflection of a very real part of myself that was spiritual in nature. Love seemed to be the kind of evidence I was looking for, in trying to substantiate the existence of spiritual things. That didn't necessarily constitute any kind of scientific evidence for spirituality, but neither love nor spirituality (nor God, for that matter) was confined to scientific or physical parameters, so maybe it was OK not to be able to prove it that way.

I started to think that any human being who really searched himself could *find* that capacity to love and to override the influence of his instincts. It was conceivable to me that my capacity to love really could be my free will— that in allowing me to remove myself from myself love would enable me to have a new perspective on what my brain was trying to make me do, so that I then had the option to evaluate and override my own impulses. I could see that in many ways, love could afford me opportunities to initiate new ideas rather than simply react to stimuli—ideas about putting my own needs and desires aside to tend to the needs of others. With love, I would be unpredictable, no longer controlled by the workings of my biological brain. With love, I would in essence have what it takes to be human. Again, there was no proof for the existence of this special entity. And yet perhaps the evidence for its being real was *just as good* as any scientific proof—the evidence simply being common human experience. Nobody who has ever truly loved or been loved would ever deny the existence of love. And it would be unfair of myself, indeed, to demand a *scientific* proof for something that existed outside of the material, sensual world, since those things could not be proved by science. Such things nevertheless were provable at some level of reality in a non-scientific way. So it was with love. So may it have been with God.

But I had never experienced God. I could believe in the entity of love because I had experienced it, but believing in God was another story. How would I ever find out the truth about God?

"God is made of the same thing that love is," Sonny said. "You can't believe in love if you haven't experienced it; likewise you won't believe in God unless you experience him. If you can believe in love as being something spiritual then even you can believe in a spiritual God. You may not be convinced yet that he *does* exist, but at least you should be able to see how he *could*."

He was right. I could see now, for the first time in my life, how God *could* exist. Now that I knew that there was at least one thing in my experience that was truly spiritual in nature, God did not seem like such a nebulous concept—if he existed, he would be as real as love was real.

THREE

The Mystery of God

He who lives in love lives in God, and God in him.

—1 John 4:16

God our protector, keep us in mind . . . for if we can be with you even one day, it is better than a thousand without you.

—Psalms 84: 10–11

A few days later we were watching a baseball game on TV in Sonny's hospital room, and out of the blue he flicked off the TV with his remote control, turned to me and asked, "Have you ever had a dog?"

"Sure." I said.

"Did you ever think about what it would have felt like to be that dog?"

I just looked at him. I had no idea what he was talking about or why he was talking about dogs in the middle of the ninth inning of a tied baseball game.

He continued: "Imagine yourself hanging around your master, watching him walk around the house picking things up, putting things down, staring at a glass mirror on the wall, making noises with his mouth into a telephone. You can't understand a word he's saying unless he says 'sit.' You can't understand how he can manipulate his hands. You can't understand why he doesn't bark when he wants something. You have no idea that he can communicate sentences and ideas with his mouth. All you know is that he feeds you and plays with you and cares for you."

"That's the way it is with God and us, only on a different level. His capabilities and his methods of doing things are a mystery to us. He's better than we are, he's different from us in many ways, like we're different from dogs. Just because we have no way of understanding him doesn't mean that we can't fully believe in his existence. Just because he's mysterious doesn't mean he isn't real."

The analogy got me thinking. I remembered a movie I had seen in college about the possibility of there being extra dimensions (in addition to length, width and depth). The idea was drawn from a book called *Flatland*, by Edwin Abbott. In the book, there was a world that existed entirely in two dimensions. Everything was two-dimensional: the world was a flat plane, the people were flat as pancakes and all the objects were flat. Part of the story involved the passage of a three-dimensional sphere through these people's two-dimensional world. The people could only see and understand in two dimensions, though, so as the sphere was passing through their world, all they could see of it at any given moment was that slice of it that was actually in the plane of their two-dimensional flat land. Their perception of the sphere, then, was a tiny circle that grew larger as the middle cross-section of the sphere approached the flatland, and then a shrinking circle that eventually vanished as the sphere passed through and away from the flatland. This was all they saw. They could not appreciate the height or depth of the sphere, only the length and width of the mysterious changing circle that they saw.

Thinking about this made me wonder if God was like that—that maybe I was only capable of seeing or understanding a part of him—and that there might be much more to him than what I was able to see. It made me realize that there were mysteries about God that I might never understand, but that didn't necessarily mean that those

39

mysteries weren't true. And yet I still hadn't been able to see the part of God that I was *supposed* to be able to experience and understand. Even in my own "dimensions" I had not yet been able to find him. As exciting as it was for me to realize how a spiritual God *could* exist, it was frustrating to know that I still had not found him.

And in a way, I was a little bit afraid of throwing my whole self into the effort of finding him. Because now that I knew that he *could* exist as a spiritual being (in some ways like me), I realized that it shouldn't be very hard for me to find him; and I couldn't help but wonder what would happen if I *didn't* find him, even after doing all the right things and exercising my own spirituality to look for him. Perhaps I would prove to myself that there *wasn't* any God. Now that I was really looking for him, I would either find him or I wouldn't. Unlike all of my previous religious efforts, this time I was going for an answer. What would I do if the answer was something that I didn't want to hear? What if there *was* no God?

"What if I do all the right things to search for God, but then never find him?" I asked him. "What happens then? Then I'll have to admit to myself that there isn't any God, and I don't know if I could take that."

"Have you ever thought about what your life would be like if you knew for sure that there wasn't any God?" he asked me.

"I have," I replied. "But to be honest with you, it scares me to death just to think about it—thinking that there might not be anyone to pray to, thinking that there might not be anything to look forward to after I die. The only possibly good thing about it is that there wouldn't be any eternal punishment to be afraid of either (I guess I'd rather be totally dead than to live through eternal punishment). So if that was the case, I could be selfish and "grab all the gusto" in life, since it would be the only life I'd ever have. But that's pretty depressing, too, don't you think? It takes all of the meaning out of life. Life wouldn't be worth much if there wasn't any reason to be good to the people you care about."

"You could still care about them."

"Well, over the last few years, I've developed a provisional plan to go into effect in case there isn't any God," I explained to him. "I'll still spend my life trying to be good to the people I love. That'll be my purpose in life—at least I'll be using my humanity while I'm alive. That's kind of been my 'backup system' for keeping myself sane if I find out that God really doesn't exist. And I depend on it. I keep trying to look for God, but as time goes on and God continues not to make himself known to me, I learn to depend on it more and more. I guess that's still the way it is. I'd love to find him if he's really out there, but if he's not, I'll still have a way of maintaining my purpose in life."

Sonny was silent for a few moments. "No wonder you've never found him," he said gently. "You've already talked yourself out of him. Your preparation for 'just in case' has been the exact opposite of faith." He paused and looked out the window for a moment then continued. "You'll never believe in God if you hang on to that. When you were a little boy, what would have happened if every time you were about to sit in a chair you had to be afraid that the chair would vanish in thin air and leave you tumbling on your backside. Or each time you took a step, that the floor was going to give way and send you hurling through the bottom of the earth into China. You'd never give the chair or the floor the chance to hold you up. You'd never sit down. You'd never take a step. You might find out sooner or later by accident that chairs and floors are solid, but then you'd still never trust them. You'd always be afraid that your next step might be your last. So you'd probably never take enough steps to learn how to walk, or to run or to jump. Likewise with God. It's OK to consider the possibility of his not being real, but to constantly be prepared for him not to exist—whether its conscious or unconscious—is to take away your chance to ever really believe in him."

"So what else can I do? I have to be honest with myself. I can't just throw away my doubts."

"You're doing more than just doubting. You've prepared yourself to *not* believe. Now I'm telling you that you have to prepare yourself *to* believe. You don't have to throw away your doubts, but you have to throw away the fear of what your doubts predict. You've braced yourself for what will happen if God doesn't exist. But when you protect yourself that way, you take away the chance for God to reach you. Believe me, you're not open to him. You'll never find him that way. If you don't find him—if you don't experience him—you'll never believe in him."

"I don't know if its worth the risk to put down those defenses, Sonny. I would lose my mind if I found out that there really was no God and I had nothing to fall back on or live for. Can you imagine that? No God, no purpose, no nothing. Just seventy miserable years and then dust. I couldn't take that. I can't even think about it."

"If you're really going to look for him, you have to be willing to risk not finding him. But at the same time, you have to prepare yourself to find him. There's more evidence than what you're able to see right now. You have to open up your soul to feel his love. You have to throw away your defenses to hear his voice and feel his touch. You've got to find that part of yourself that's spiritual like he is, and let nothing get in the way of your using it. Not your fears, not your defenses, not your doubts." He paused for a moment. "One thing I can promise you," he continued, "is that a chance to find God is worth the risk."

FOUR

Reasons to Believe in God

The idea that space and time may form a closed surface without boundary has profound implications for the role of God in the affairs of the universe. With the success of scientific theories in describing events, most people have come to believe that God allows the universe to evolve according to a set of laws and does not intervene in the universe to break these laws. However, the laws do not tell us what the universe should have looked like when it started—it would still be up to God to wind up the clockwork and choose how to start it off. So long as the universe had a beginning, we could suppose it had a creator. But if the universe is really completely self-contained, having no boundary or edge, it would have neither beginning nor end: it would simply be. What place, then, for a creator?

—*Stephen W. Hawking, physicist,*
in A BRIEF HISTORY OF TIME

God does not play dice.
—*Albert Einstein, in response to profound implications of*
the Heisenberg Uncertainty Principle, which postulates that
the universe is governed ultimately by random occurences

"So you think," I said, "that all the people in the world who really believe in God must have actually experienced him somehow."

"Of course. Otherwise he wouldn't be real to anybody."

43

"I don't know, Sonny. I think people have all kinds of reasons for *believing* in God. Some people have tried to philosophically *prove* his existence. That he's the uncaused cause, or the epitome of being, without which nothing else could exist. If you could prove God, you wouldn't have to 'experience' him to know that he's real."

"Proof about God can only be theoretical," he answered. "Experience is real."

"It's hard for me to imagine that all the millions of people who believe in God have experienced God. I went to religious schools, went to church, tried to find him all my life—how could I have missed him when so many other people seem to have found him?"

"There's a big difference between people who believe in God and people who *say* they believe in God."

"What do you mean?" I asked him.

"I mean that a lot of the people out there who say they believe in God don't have a very clear idea about *why* they believe in God. So how can they really believe in him? They can believe in traditions or stories that have been handed down to them by their families, or by what they read in books. But that's not belief in God. That's not knowing who God is. There are a lot of people who say they believe in God, and in the same breath might talk about how much they hate somebody. People who go to church for an hour a week after they've spent every other hour of the week living a selfish or destructive life. Do you think that they know God? Do you think that God is real to them? If they really knew God, if they *knew* he was with them like you're with me right now, standing here in the flesh—which is what believing is really all about—they wouldn't live their lives the way they do."

"You're saying that they're hypocrites."

"I guess I am. But it's not their fault," he said. "They don't know any better. They say they believe in God because that's the thing to do. They *want* to believe that there is a God. Or even if they don't, they think it'll get them out of going to hell or something. I'm telling you, if all those people who say they believe in God really *did* believe in God, this world would be a totally different place. So don't think that so many people have something that you don't have. You'll find him. Everybody can find him. They just have to look for him in the right ways. The problem is that not everybody's willing to do what it takes to find him the right way. It can be risky opening your heart up to God if you have to let go of material things to do it. Especially when you're looking for someone you might not find right away. As you said, it's scary to even look for him and risk the disappointment of not finding him if you're afraid that he might not be there. A lot of people would rather be content with their personal opinion that there's a God in heaven, and leave it at that. So they settle for less and end up with a faith that's useless—a faith that can't motivate them out of a wet paper bag. Real faith moves mountains. That's the kind of faith you want to live by. You should be thankful that you haven't settled for something less than that."

"So if what you're saying is true, why do so many people *think* they believe in God when they really don't?"

"Most of the time they just settle for bad reasons to believe in God, and they never realize how bad their reasons are. Let's face it, deep down almost everybody *wants* to believe that God exists, so some people are going to believe in him whether they have good evidence or not. They'll just convince themselves that whatever evidence they have is good enough, and they go on 'believing' in what really doesn't amount to anything more than a fantasy. Other people may try to be more honest with themselves about not being able to reach a conclusion about God, but they sometimes get influenced by the idea that it's much safer to believe in God than to not believe in God."

"What do you mean by 'safer'?" I asked him.

"Well, there's this calculation you can do about God that goes something like this: If God *exists,* and you *believe* in him, you have a shot at eternal life. If God *exists,* and you *don't believe* in him, he might send you to hell (if you believe that that's how God operates). If God *doesn't exist,* it doesn't matter whether you believe in him or not; you just die and that's it. So when you put it all together, even if you only think there's a slight possibility that God exists, the best bet is just to 'believe' in him: that way, you have everything to gain and nothing to lose. If you decide *not* to believe in him, you have nothing to gain and everything to lose, because if he does turn out to be real, then you go to hell.

"Obviously," he continued, "this has nothing to do with believing in God. It's more like gambling. The only reason I'm bringing it up is that I think it might be operating at some level in a lot of people's minds to help them *think* they believe in God, even when they really don't." He paused for a moment, then went on. "If you questioned all the people you know who say they believe in God, and asked them *why* they believe in God, what do you think they'd say? I'll bet half of them would tell you that they believe in God because *somebody* must have created the world and all the stars and everything, so it must have been God. That's no reason to believe in God. They don't believe in God. And they're not going to *act* like they believe in God, they just think they do and say that they do."

"You don't think that's a good reason, about God creating the world?"

"No way. Haven't you ever heard of evolution? You don't need God to explain why the natural world is what it is. That's what science is for, to explain those things. The Big Bang. Natural Selection. It's all there in the textbooks. Luckily science has taken away a lot of bad reasons for believing in God." He paused for a moment. "If God was just our explanation for things we couldn't understand, there wouldn't be anything real to go on. Who's to say God didn't create the world zillions of years ago and then die? Even if he did create the world it doesn't necessarily mean that he's still around. It's just no good to base your faith on an unexplainable event or on some ancient mystery. You have to justify your belief in a God who lives now—a God who's with you in this very room."

"So you're shooting down thousands of people's reason for believing in God just like that."

"I'm not saying God didn't create the world. I happen to believe that he *did*. But that's not *why* I believe in him. I've got much better reasons than that to believe in him. Once I knew him and was able to understand him, then it was easy to see how somebody like him could have created the world. But the belief and understanding come first. Not the explanation for the world."

"I guess science can explain away lots of things that people used to attribute to God."

"Anybody whose faith is shaken by science doesn't really have faith. Science can't say anything about God, either to prove him or to disprove him. Science can only deal with things that we can see and hear and touch and taste and smell—that's what makes it science. God can't be perceived by those mechanisms. He's spiritual." He stopped to think a moment. "Once you believe in God, then science can help you *appreciate* some of the things he might have done in creating the world. Even though life evolved on its own, did you ever think about the forces and laws that all of nature abides by? Electrical and magnetic force, gravity, space, time—the things that govern the physical world. Maybe God used building blocks like atoms and molecules and those basic laws and forces to design a system that would carry out his creation on its own. Imagine what it would take to design a system that could produce things as massive as planets or as intricate as hummingbirds by interacting with itself and evolving. And imagine creating it with something so simple as lifeless matter and a few profound laws of nature. Complexity from simplicity. Variety from uniformity. Life from lifelessness. If you believe that God was responsible for it all, it makes you respect him and admire him all the more. But you can't base your faith on that—

those are just ideas, ways of thinking about a God who you have to understand in other more important ways first."

"How can I understand him if I can't even find him?"

"You haven't looked hard enough," Sonny said. "He's all around you."

"Where is he? It isn't so obvious that he's all around, you know. It's a pretty disgusting world out there." Once again, I began to think about the people of Auschwitz, and the poor of the world. How could any of them hang onto their belief in God? In a way, it made me feel obnoxious to be questioning God on the basis of my own minor disappointments, because so many of those horribly persecuted people *did* hang on to their faith. How they did it, I couldn't understand. Maybe part of it had to do with the fact that God was a life-and-death reality to them; to me, he had never been any more than a philosophical argument. So who was I to question the consensus of the greater part of all humankind? Hindus, Jews, Catholics all over the world gasping for their last breath with God on their lips. And now I was trying to decide essentially if all of them were right or all of them were wrong. Why was it, I wondered, that so many people all over the world believed in God, when it was so hard for me to believe in him? In a way, it made me feel like I was missing something. Or was it that *they* were missing something and it was all just a big lie. Could *that* many people be that badly deceived about something so important?

I knew that there were lots of reasons why people believed in God, some good reasons, some not-so-good reasons. What made me most suspicious of poor or persecuted people's reasons was that I knew how badly they must have *wanted* God to exist. They had nothing else but God to comfort them or give them hope for a better life, or ease their suffering. No doubt, to need God that badly would influence anybody's decision on whether or not to believe in him. As Sonny was saying, it would make people believe in him no matter what the evidence for his existence was, for reasons they'd probably never accept in any other argument. Needing God badly would obviously be a bad reason to believe in him, but if they were poor, it would only be human to do that. Maybe Karl Marx was right when he said that there was nothing real about God and that religion was just a fantasy that served to comfort the masses. Religion, to him, was nothing more than a predictable human "reaction" to desperation, almost like an animal instinct. A sort of knee-jerk reflex of the human mind to soften the impact of adversity when one had no power to escape or defend against it. Which would explain why the most desperate people would be the ones who seemed to believe in God the most.

Except for one thing. I had been around enough religious people in my life to know that people who really loved God didn't love him *because* he was going to get them out of some kind of mess, or *because* they would go to heaven after they died. They loved God because they loved God. It usually wasn't a situation in which they wanted something in return for their devotion. Their devotion was a consequence of their understanding of God, not the other way around—their understanding of God didn't seem to be dictated by the need to devote themselves to a higher being. This isn't what you would expect from people who are believing in God out of desperation. And this alone made me consider the possibility that there might be more to the uniqueness of the faithful poor than just their desperation. What if, instead of making God up, they could actually *see* God better than anybody else could. What if their simplicity or their destitution or their suffering somehow made them *more capable* of sensing the influence or existence of a real God than anyone else could. The poor might have been more free to give themselves to God, since there weren't so many worldly things to distract their devotion. Perhaps, then, there was a secret in their simplicity that allowed them to experience God more fully, and to find in that experience unquestionable evidence for his existence. By being able to open their hearts better, they would be better able to find God. The strength of their belief would be a consequence of the experience. Maybe Sonny was right about the importance of experiencing God.

I asked him again, more out of desperation than anything else, how I would find God in a world of selfishness and destruction and death.

"He's in all of those things just as much as he is in the love two people have for one another. He suffers with us, he loves us so much. You've got to look for him. I think you're ready. Look harder. The only way to believe in him—to really believe in him—is to know him and feel him touch you. And he will touch you. As soon as you feel that touch, you have the beginning of faith. When you have that you'll want to learn more about him. As you learn more about him you'll feel him touch you more. It's a 'vicious cycle.' He will burn inside of you if you let him touch you and do everything you can to know him better. And you'll surely grow to love him with more love than you've ever known."

"To love him who is the essence of love," I said. "I want to believe you, Sonny. God, I want to believe you."

"You need to understand him more. The only way to understand God is to understand his love."

FIVE

Raison d'être

. . . . If I have faith in all its fullness, to move mountains, but without love, then I am nothing at all. If I give away all that I possess, piece by piece, and if I even let them take my body to burn it, but am without love, it will do me no good whatever.

—*1 Corinthians 13: 2–3*

Anyone who fails to love can never have known God, because God is love.

—*1 John 4:8*

In retrospect, it was difficult for me to think of God in terms of love because at that time in my life I had isolated myself enough in my work and my career that very little love got through to me. Not that I wasn't loved; I just didn't feel it. I was too busy and too independent. It's easy to forget what love is like when you keep it away from yourself all the time.

There was one person in my life at that time whose love did get through to me in spite of my defenses—her name was Ruth. We had been dating on and off for about two years. She lived alone in an apartment on the other side of town, and although she had other friends, she kept to herself most of the time when she wasn't working or with me. She was one of those "still waters run deep" kind of people—quiet, an intense listener and observer, and almost mysterious in an exciting kind of way—even after dating her for two years I knew very little about her other friends or her past because she never talked about them. When she was with me she only wanted to talk about things that concerned the two of us.

What I did know about her was that she came from a poor family, and that she left home when she was about seventeen, at the beginning of her senior year in high school, for reasons that she would never really go into (no matter how many times I asked her), but that had partly to do with her not wanting to be a financial burden on her family, according to her. She somehow got herself through school, and when I met her she was twenty years old, working as a cashier in a grocery store near my apartment, taking college classes at night.

I was enormously attracted to her from the day I met her, not only because she was physically beautiful, but because she was one of those exceptional people who are both soft and strong at the same time. She was quiet, but the feelings she expressed in her silences were every bit as deep and meaningful as those she put into words. Whenever she spoke, you knew it was coming from her heart— you could hear it in her voice and see it in her eyes. Anyway, despite how much I thought I loved her, it always bothered me that her past was so shrouded in mystery. I always had the feeling that I didn't know something I probably ought to know. All kinds of crazy things used to go through my mind: perhaps she had been abused or something, I would think to myself, (why else would she have run away from home?), or somehow psychologically damaged from growing up in a terrible neighborhood. Maybe she would turn on me one day or be callous in some fundamental way I couldn't yet see. Perhaps desperation or bitterness or anger were in her blood or her genes or somehow deeply ingrained in her from what her past had been like. Whatever I thought it might be, it had little or nothing to do with how she really was toward me. These were just unsubstantiated fears of mine, which I never really had the heart or the guts to share with her, and which prevented me from committing myself to her in anywhere near the degree to which she committed herself to me.

Over the course of two years we fell in love, but ever so cautiously, and there were many times when the tensions generated from my underlying fears nearly tore us apart. I pushed Ruth away a lot because of those fears, and she clung to me too much in spite of them. My feelings of being "closed in" and her feelings of being desperate were a part of our love. So at that time my idea of what love was all about, even as it applied to understanding God, was intimately enmeshed in my understanding of what was happening to Ruth and me, and the concept of love conjured up enough mixed messages to make me miss the point of a lot of what Sonny had said about God and love.

I remember especially one night about two weeks after I had first seen Sonny in the hospital. Ruth and I were sitting around at her apartment having had dinner together, and she was in an unusually talkative mood. Out of the blue she asked me,

"Do you love me, John?"

"Yes, I do love you," I said. It was almost a reflex. She had taken me by surprise.

"Why?"

"What do you mean, *why?*" I asked her.

"Why do you love me?"

"I don't understand why you're asking me that—you know I love you."

"I want to know *why,*" she persisted.

"Well," I replied, "why do *you* think I love you."

"I don't know. That's why I asked you." She looked away and smiled. "Is it something physical . . . or do I intellectually stimulate you . . . or what?"

"Why are you asking me this?"

"I want to know," she said firmly.

"Why do I love you. . . ." I stalled as I grappled for the right words, ". . . OK, let's see. . . . I've always thought that you're strong inside—stronger than I am, and I love that about you . . . and you've got a lot of guts living on your own the way you have . . . and I love being with you—you always try to make me feel good . . . and I think that you're gorgeous and that definitely helps. . . ."

"So you admire me and I'm nice to you and you like the way I look. Why do you **love** me?"

"I love almost everything about you—all those things go into it—they're what make you *you*."

"But those 'things' don't mean anything. *They can change.* Love isn't supposed to change . . . so it shouldn't depend on things that can change."

"What do you mean?"

"What if I change? What if I get old and ugly. Would you still love me?"

"Sure," I answered, "why wouldn't I?"

"Maybe you'd think, *'that's not the person I fell in love with—the person I fell in love with was physically beautiful—this is a different person.'* It happens all the time you know; people stop loving one another because their looks change."

"Don't worry, Ruth. I would still love you."

"All right then what if I got into a car accident and got crippled or something?"

"It wouldn't matter. I'd still love you."

"What if something happened to me that made my mind fall apart so that I wasn't so nice to you any more or I wasn't intellectually stimulating any more—like if I got mentally ill or something. Then what?"

That was something I had to think about before I could answer right away. "I guess that would be harder to take. . . ." I stopped and wondered what it was that she was getting at. Rather than trying to *understand* where she was coming from, I began to *worry* again about her mysterious past and what kind of a person she was that she would ask me such a strange question. I was starting to get suspicious of her and felt like I had to be careful. I honestly wondered if she somehow had the idea that she herself was on the brink of some big change, and if she was trying to get me to make some kind of commitment to her before it happened. "Part of why I love you," I steadily continued, "is the way your mind works and the way you are to me. I suppose it would depend on why your mind was changing—if it was something that was happening to you that you had no control over, or if you were doing it on purpose."

"You think I'd let my mind fall apart on purpose?"

"No, I guess not," I answered.

"So if my mind started to slip, who would be the judge of whether I was doing it on purpose or not?"

"Only you could be the judge of that," I said.

"But *you* would have to make the decision on whether or not to keep loving me, so you would have to decide whether or not I was in control of my changing mind." She was quiet for a moment and then a sort of desperate look came over her face. "Can I tell you something, John?" she continued. "If I *ever* start acting like I don't love you any more, it will be because I've lost my mind—that would be the only reason. That's how much I love you. . . . I would never in my right mind stop loving you. I want you to know that. That won't ever change."

I didn't know what to say. There was a long silence.

"Promise me you wouldn't stop loving me if I lost my mind. It wouldn't be fair if you stopped. It wouldn't be my fault." By now she had almost a look of terror in her eyes. Now I was *really* getting scared of her. The whole thing was just getting too weird.

"Do you plan on losing your mind in the near future?" I nervously joked.

"NO!" she snapped, and pushed herself away from me to the opposite end of the couch we were sitting on. "But it could happen to anyone—even you, Mr. All-American. You don't understand, do you. Do you know what happens when people start to lose their mind? They lose control of

55

their own thoughts, and it's not their fault, they can't help it. If they want to think about their job, or someone they love, or how to make dinner, they can't do it because their mind is out of control . . . instead they're possessed by their damaged brains, obsessed with themselves, with their temptations, with crazy ideas . . . thoughts come in and out as they please—thoughts that are forced on them, over which they have no control. Can you think of anything more horrible than that? How would you like to be abandoned if that happened to you?"

"You're right, Ruth, I'm sorry." I'd never thought much about losing my mind before. There was a long silence. "Life can be pretty scary for all kinds of reasons, can't it?" At that point something happened that to this day stands out in my mind, although Ruth probably didn't think twice about it. In an awkward attempt to share what she was going through, I moved back next to her on the couch and put my arm around her. I'm positive that most girls would have moved away from me in that situation, because it was incredibly awkward the way I did it. And yet Ruth could look beyond that—she knew that even though I didn't understand her, I wanted to be there for her when she was scared—and that's what was important to her. That was one of the extraordinary things about her—it never really mattered to her if I agreed with her or not, just that I was *with her* in her most difficult moments. She kissed me to make me feel less awkward, and put her head on my shoulder, and at that moment more than at any other time, I realized why I loved her. I should have told her that, but I was afraid to talk about loving her any more because I was afraid of what I was getting myself into. I didn't love her *enough* to accept that part of her that I didn't understand. I was afraid that in the long run it would hurt me.

After a few minutes I asked her, "Did you ever know anybody who lost their mind?"

Not really," she said softly.

"I have to be honest with you, Ruth," I said, "it would be hard for me to keep loving somebody who was out of their mind."

"If you stopped loving them because they were out of their mind, then you never really loved them in the first place. Love isn't some kind of a faucet that you turn on and off. If your love is real it's always on. No matter what happens. It's unconditional. It's not like you can say, *I love you "if" this or "if" that.* You love somebody no matter what happens to them or you don't love them."

"But when people lose their minds—even if they go just a little bit crazy—they aren't the same person any more," I said.

"That's nonsense," she said sharply. "When people change like that, it's not their fault. Do you think anybody wants to change so that their loved ones won't love them any more? Their changes are a part of them. We all change in this life—some of us more, some of us less, some for better, some for worse—that's part of being human. Those changes are a part of us. We're still the same person whether we or anybody else likes it or not. We're stuck with ourselves. I think it's cruel to think, *'Oh well, I don't have to love you any more because you turned into a different person.'* That's a bunch of bull."

"People aren't robots, Ruth. They have free will."

"Not when their minds go bad, they don't—when it comes to that, their minds are out of control. They can't even concentrate long enough to be in touch with any free will."

"You think so?"

"How *could* you have free will if you couldn't even keep your mind on the things you wanted to think about? Whether you're depressed or addicted or obsessed or just plain nuts, your mind is out of control. When your mind gets preoccupied with things that you don't have any control over, your free will gets buried. Not that you aren't human any more, but you're a victim of something you can't control. Nobody *chooses* to go out of control or lose their free will—it just happens. And once you've buried your free will, how can you *willfully choose* to get it back?"

I immediately recalled the conversation I had had with Sonny about self-awareness and free will and those aspects of our humanity that keep us from being controlled completely by our brains. Now Ruth was exploring the ultimate consequence of the loss of that free will, and it was starting to scare me as much as it was scaring her. I inwardly wondered if it was possible for *love* to resurrect a failing free will when the latter was being dominated by an out-of-control brain.

When she mentioned the point about "your mind gets preoccupied," it reminded me, too, of what the old monk had told me about why he chose to be poor. He wanted to keep his heart from getting cluttered with things that would distract him from loving (and being loved by) God. To him, when the mind was preoccupied, his ability to love went away. To Ruth, free will went away. Sonny would have agreed with both of them—man's free will and his ability to love were very closely tied together (if not one in the same) according to him. It occurred to me that perhaps "becoming preoccupied" with all of the material things of this world (thereby forfeiting the ability to look beyond oneself and love) was a *voluntary* way of giving up one's own free will—which is exactly what happens *involuntarily* to someone who loses their mind. In that case, the temptation to become "materially preoccupied" might be every bit as dangerous as the threat of becoming mentally ill. I could see how materialism (in any one of its many forms) could get to be a kind of vicious cycle: as it starts to take over, it overrides free will; the less free will you have, the less ability to take your mind off of the material things that continually try to preoccupy it. Instinctual desires, selfish tendencies, the lure of the material world . . . all of these could take over in almost the same way that mental illness conquers the mind and heart. Maybe it was true that the secret of the faith of *poor* people had to do with a lack of such distractions, making them more free to seek and experience the love of God.

I could easily see how the kinds of things that take away a person's free will might at the same time take away their ability to love. If you loved somebody who gave up their free will (voluntarily or involuntarily) could your love penetrate their preoccupation and "win them back"? Was love that powerful? I still wondered whether or not it was even possible to love somebody who couldn't love you back. I knew deep down that Ruth would have loved me regardless of whether or not I loved her back, but I wasn't so sure that I could say the same for myself. When I think back on that conversation, I remember how worried I was that she might be telling me that she was about to lose her mind. Rather than try and help her with that, I was afraid to get any more involved with her than I already was. In a sense, I didn't want to love her any more. So I felt bad about myself— embarrassed, and kind of cold—sitting there next to her, realizing that part of me didn't want to have anything to do with her. We sat in silence for a long time. As perverse as it sounds, I began to try to think of ways to talk her out of loving me so I could somehow get myself off the hook, as far as our relationship was concerned.

"Maybe I'm changing," I finally said to her. "I guess ever since I went to college. . . . I think I'm a more *calculating* person than I used to be. . . ."

"You grew up, John, that's all. The older you get, the more complicated life gets, and you have to deal with it. You *have* to be calculating in a way."

I stopped to think. "It's more than that, though," I told her. "I don't know. . . . This is going to sound weird but I don't cry any more." I was telling the truth, and it was something that had bothered me about myself for a long time. "I can't remember when was the last time I cried.

Even when I feel like I should, like at funerals and things. It makes me think I'm not really human any more. It kind of makes me think there's something wrong with me."

"You're a big tough macho man, that's all," Ruth replied, trying to rescue me with a smile.

"No really, Ruth. I don't think I could cry if I wanted to. Doesn't that scare you about me?"

"Whenever people cry," she softly answered, "they're crying for themselves. When somebody dies, if you really love them, a part of you dies too. If they're not a part of you, you probably never really loved them. If you never really loved them, and they're not a part of you, there's no reason to cry." She stopped to think. "Most of the time people just cry because they feel sorry for themselves. Maybe you never feel sorry for yourself. There's nothing wrong with that."

"I feel sorry for myself sometimes. I know that. But I don't believe what you're saying about people only crying for themselves. I think people can cry for other people without crying for themselves."

"People only cry when they've been hurt themselves," she persisted. "If something happens to somebody else, it all depends on how much they mean to you. If that other person means so much to you that they're a *part* of you, then sure you're going to cry. If they're not a part of you, you won't cry. Why should you? What makes people cry is that part of themselves is lost or hurt or damaged because of what happens to a person that they really love."

"How do you know, Ruth?"

"I just do."

"How do you know so much about crying?" I asked her.

"When you do enough of it yourself, you learn all about it. I've cried more than my fair share . . . and it's always been for myself. Let me tell you, it's not such a great thing. Don't feel so bad that you don't do it." She looked at me squarely and said, "It's probably better to be so strong that you don't *need* anybody to be a part of you. That way you don't get hurt if they let you down or they go away or they die."

"Do *you* need somebody to be a part of you?" I asked her.

"Only the people I love," she said.

"Tell me the truth," I said. "What is it that's made you cry more than your fair share?"

"I'm human," she said, "and you break my heart on a regular basis. I've been waiting for you to get up the guts to propose to me, and you can't even figure out whether you love me or not." You could have heard a pin drop. Then she laughed in a delightfully attractive kind of way that I can't begin to describe, except by describing my relief at knowing that she was only kidding. At least I was pretty sure that she was only kidding. Still, I was disturbed that she couldn't answer me honestly about whatever it was that she cried so much about.

She reached for my hand and smiled, "I'm sorry, John. I didn't mean to make you feel bad. You've always been good to me. I just wanted to get your attention." With some degree of effort, she maintained the smile that remained after the laugh wore off. "I was only kidding. I don't cry that much. Really. I don't know why I said it."

Somehow I knew she was lying.

SIX

The Love of God

Come to me, all you who labor and are overburdened, and I will give you rest. Shoulder my yoke and learn from me, for I am gentle and humble in heart, and you will find rest for your souls. Yes, my yoke is easy and my burden light.

—*Matthew 11: 28–30*

"Lord, how often must I forgive my brother if he wrongs me? As often as seven times?" He replied, "Not seven, I tell you, but seventy *times* seven times."

—*Matthew 18:21–22*

A man can have no greater love than to lay down his life for his friends.

—*John 15:13*

I was so worried about what I didn't know about Ruth that I failed to fully realize the magnificence of what I *did* know about her. Deep down I wanted to love her more than my brain would let me, but I wasn't in touch with that at the time. My fears about Ruth were like some *giant toothache* that completely preoccupied me. When you have a bad toothache, all you can think about is your tooth. It's hard to concentrate on anything else, or feel anything else, and it's almost impossible to hear the quiet whispers of pleasure or goodness or reassurance over the screaming pain in your tooth.

I think the truth was that aside from all of my worries about her past, Ruth threatened my independence. She was a very *needy* kind of person. The longer I knew her, the more sure I had become that, aside from the general desperation of whatever her family circumstances had been, she was very insecure about her own worth. It had taken her a long time to be able to believe me when I told her how much I thought of her, and until she could, she never really trusted me in general. But when she finally *was* able to trust me, she handed herself over to me as if she were giving me the greatest gift she could come up with—yet at the same time afraid that I might not like it.

She was always careful not to show me any of her weaknesses, and that really turned me off, because I could have loved her even for her weaknesses—it was just the unknown that I couldn't tolerate. It's much easier to love a weak person than to love somebody who keeps you in the dark, even if they look better on the surface. Whenever I pulled away from her though, she would just cling to me all the more tightly, showering me with devotion, subjecting herself to whatever pain my resistance could impose—all in an effort to hang on, because she thought she needed me. What she needed was for someone to show her what she deserved to know, which was that she was good and strong and wonderful. But I was too afraid to get close enough to her to show her. All in all, after that night's conversation, I was left with a sense of confusion about her, and about love in general. And I had no idea how love would get me anywhere near God.

A few days later, I went to see Sonny and told him all about the conversation that Ruth and I had had, and about the things that were troubling me. I told him that I felt afraid to love her, that I didn't understand her, and that I was very uneasy about all the things she said about the prospect of losing her mind. After patiently hearing everything I had to say, he simply turned to me and said, "She's right."

"What do you mean, 'she's right'?" I said. I felt a little betrayed and angry at him.

"You see, you've got to get it through your head that love is unconditional or else it isn't love. For some reason, you're not getting it."

"What's that supposed to mean?"

"I want you to try something for me. Close your eyes and picture Ruth in your mind. . . . her hair, her eyes, her face—picture in your mind all the things you love about her: the way she smiles, the way she walks, the kinds of things she does—everything you love about her. Are you doing that?"

"I am."

"Now let's suppose that one of her qualities—one of those things that you love about her—went away. Would you still love her?"

"Of course I would," I said.

"Of course you would." He reiterated. "Now let's say that one by one the rest of those qualities that you love about her started to be taken away. If five of them were missing would you still love her?"

"Sure," I answered.

"How about ten? Think about it. Does your love for her change as each quality is taken away?"

Now the picture in my mind was changing. "It's bound to change," I said. "Why would you think it wouldn't change? Those are the things I love about her."

"If your love changes, it isn't love," he replied very deliberately. "Love is *unconditional*. If you really loved this girl, it would mean that if her face got wrinkled or she was unkind to you, or if for some reason she started to forget things, or got some crazy ideas, you would still love her just the same. If you could make it clear to her that she doesn't have to act a certain way to hang onto your love, then she'll let you know who she really is, and you'll be able to love *the real her*. But until she understands that from you, don't expect her ever to give up her secrets. She'll never tell you any of the bad things about herself—she'll never let you know who she really is unless she knows your love is constant and unconditional."

"Love is unconditional," he continued. "Its not a matter of saying, 'I'll scratch your back if you scratch mine'— it's not a contract or a reflex. It's a matter of saying, 'I'll scratch your back no matter what you do to me. I'll think of you. I'll care about you. I'll support you. I'll laugh with you when you feel like laughing. I'll cry with you when you're crying. And I'll never stop, no matter what happens to you.' That's what God's love is like. And we're all capable of loving each other in just that same way."

"It sounds great, Sonny, but who really loves anybody like that? Nobody's perfect. How can you be 'yourself' and love somebody if there are things about them that really turn you off?"

"You have to be honest with yourself that they turn you off, but you have to love them in spite of it. That's what makes love different from just an emotion or a feeling. It's more a commitment or a devotion to a person than anything else. And when your love is strong enough, those things that turn you off about the other person aren't nearly as important as the whole human being that you're trying to love."

"Even if I *was* able to love Ruth that way," I said, "I still don't think it would do us any good. I'll bet she still wouldn't be herself."

"Don't be so sure."

"You're telling me to love her enough so she can feel good about being herself. But if she can't be herself in the first place, how can I begin to love her? I don't even know who she really is. It's a vicious cycle."

"So you have two choices," he said, and smiled. "You can either continue to fake each other out with false appearances and conditional love, *or* one of you can wave the white flag."

"What do you mean?" I asked him.

"One of you has to surrender yourself to the other person. She either has to be 'herself' completely so you can love her, or you have to love her so she can be herself. If you really want something to happen, you're the one that's going to have to make the first move."

"All right," I said. "Let's just say for argument's sake that I was dumb enough to do that. Let's say I decide to commit myself to Ruth no matter who she is. Do you think she'd really believe me enough to trust me with her secrets? How would I even get her to believe that I really feel the way I do?"

"That's the catch. You have to trust her with *your* secrets first. You have to let her see your weaknesses. You have to make yourself just as vulnerable as she is so she won't feel threatened by you. You have to love her so much that you can't do without her. Then she'll trust you. But you have to be strong enough to *give up* your strength and put your whole self in her hands. If you can do that, then she'll let you love the real Ruth. As it stands now, though, she doesn't think she's good enough for you. Unless you convince her otherwise, nothing's going to change."

"So in order to convince her," I grudgingly concluded, "I *have* to make myself vulnerable to her."

"The ultimate act of love is to make yourself vulnerable."

"So how do I go about making myself vulnerable to her? Do I just tell her what all of my weaknesses are? I can't see how that by itself will do much good."

"Now we're getting somewhere," he said as he smiled. "You're right, there *is* one other thing that you have to do besides letting her know who you really are. **You have to let her love you.**"

What does *that* mean?"

"Ruth loves you very much, but you don't *let* her love

you. You're afraid of her so you push her away. Let her love you. Let her scratch your back, so to speak. Let yourself be carried by her love—she loves you more than you're even capable of feeling right now. Put yourself in her arms and entrust your whole self to her."

"But what happens if she changes or tries to take advantage of me?"

"That's always a risk. But just letting her know that you're willing to take a risk like that (because you love her so much) goes a long way. You never know what can happen. Nobody said this was easy. If she chooses to take advantage of you, if she lets you fall instead of holding you up, then *she's* thrown away your trust. Let her throw away the chance to love and be loved, but don't you do it. At least you've given her the chance. That's all you can do. Believe me, if you give her a real chance, I don't think she'll throw it away."

"I wish I could believe you," I said.

"You see," he said, "the truth is that both of you have the same problem. You can't fully love because you can't let yourselves *be* loved. Sometimes that's the hardest part." He was quiet for a moment. "You know," he continued, "that's exactly what keeps most people from ever finding God. Not letting him love you. Not feeling the intensity of an infinite love that we never deserved and refuse to believe in because we can't see it. We don't want to depend on it because we can't be sure how real it is so most of us never even give ourselves a chance to experience it. What a slap in God's face that is for him to love us the way he does, even to the point of making himself completely vulnerable to us as a man, and then for us to turn our back on him and say, '*No thanks. We just don't understand you very well. We'd rather stick with things that are more of a sure bet.*'

"Anyway," he went on, "both of you have protected yourselves from being loved by one another. It's impossible right now for you to feel how good love can make you feel because you're protecting yourselves against how bad a broken love would feel. Pardon the analogy, and no offense intended, but you remind me of a couple of moles."

"A couple of what?"

"Moles."

"What do you mean?" I had no idea what he was talking about.

"Have you ever seen a mole?" he asked.

"You mean the little animals that dig up back yards and live underground?"

He nodded in reply.

"No," I said. "I've never seen one. Have you?" I don't even know why I asked him.

"No, I haven't either. How could I?—they always stay in their holes."

"So why are we talking about moles?"

"If you were a male mole and a female mole called you on the phone and told you she loved you, would you believe her?"

"That's ridiculous."

"Don't be a mole." He gave me a sort of stern look, then smiled.

"Sonny, what are you talking about?"

"We're all like moles sometimes. We're afraid to come out of our tunnels—to let go of our defenses, and let others see us how we really are. We're afraid they'll try to kill us. Or they'll tell us how ugly we are. So it's best just to stay in the hole." He paused for a moment, then continued. "But if we stay in the hole, we never see the light of day. We'll never feel what its like to stand defenseless and petrified outside the hole, while we let a little boy—who's just as scared—approach us cautiously, and then pick us up and pet us and protect us himself and become our closest friend. If we stay in our holes, all we ever know is darkness—we can't even see our own bodies or learn enough about ourselves to love ourselves. We can only survive. And in that case, what can we expect if on only a rare occasion we peek out of our hole to see what's happening—why is it any surprise if people

68

look at us suspiciously or withdraw from us, or take advantage of us on that rare moment.

"The mole," he continued, "is a wonderful survivor. But he leads an extraordinarily empty life. The hole protects him not only from what is bad about life, but also from what's good. You can't just filter out the bad things when you're building a defense for yourself. If it's a hole, you don't see light. If it's a wall, the people who love you can't get in. If its a tough outer shell, you can't be sensitive to feelings and emotions that make life rich and meaningful. If it's a drug, it may take away the pain, but it also makes you so numb that you can't feel the good things in life. So you have to choose. You either open yourself up to everything, or you feel nothing. If you choose to feel nothing, all you can do is survive. If you're a mole, not only is it impossible to be loved, but it's impossible to love." He was silent for a few moments. "The correct answer to my original question of the phone call from the mole," he added, "would be *not* to believe her if she told you she loved you."

I had to laugh, and he did too. "Let's put this back into real terms," I said. "Let's say that I'm going to try to love somebody who's nasty or hateful. You're telling me that I have to open myself up for them to take advantage of me, so that they can love the 'real me' if they decide to do that."

"Exactly."

"That's crazy. They'll just take advantage."

"They probably will, the first couple of times you open yourself up to them. They won't know what to do with you. People who are hateful and nasty don't get a chance to love very often because nobody ever opens up to them. Their hatefulness makes other people hate them. So they hate more, and it becomes a vicious cycle. The only way to break the vicious cycle is to love. And love will start a cycle of its own. You love them, they feel better about themselves, they try to love you, you let them—which makes them feel even better about themselves that somebody would trust them and be vulnerable to them in spite of their track record, and so on. It snowballs. The only way it starts, though, is when *you* make yourself vulnerable to that other person. You have to give your*self* to that other person. Otherwise you're not really giving them anything. You have to let them love you."

"I'm telling you, Sonny, that's taking a big risk. And for what? It's too painful when it doesn't work out."

"Sure it's painful sometimes, but it's more important to feel *something*, even if it's bad, than to throw away your chance of feeling *anything* by protecting yourself from love. Love is what makes you human, remember? It'll make you strong if you let it work within you. Strength from vulnerability . . . this is the great mystery of love. The poor know all about this mystery; they're always vulnerable. And as bad as that can be, it helps them to open their hearts to the love of their families, their friends and their God, which is what keeps them going even in the most hopeless situations. *Strength from vulnerability,* this is one of the great secrets of life."

"Is it ever possible to love someone without being vulnerable to them?" I asked him.

"If you're not vulnerable," he replied, "you can't be loved. If you can't let yourself be loved, then you can't really love. The nature of love is such that it doesn't get anywhere unless you allow it to fill you up and carry you. If you aren't vulnerable, love can't get into your heart."

Once again I recalled the old monk's words about letting the love of God fill his heart, and I started to wonder if maybe he and Sonny were using love as almost a sort of brainwash. As if love was supposed to sweep them off their feet and completely take over. I understood how important love was in terms of a person's free will, but the way they were talking about being consumed by love almost made it sound like some kind of an obsession. Some people get obsessed with money, I thought to myself, others with power, but Sonny and the old monk get obsessed with love. What's so great about that, I wondered.

After I tried to cautiously explain to him what I was thinking, I finally came out and asked him, "When you talk about being filled with love, what makes you think you're not just trading one obsession for another? Because if that's all it is, who's to say that any one person's obsession is better than another's?"

"You're concentrating on the words and you're forgetting the meaning of what love is." He took a minute or two to think. "In almost any way you look at it," he finally replied, "love is the opposite of obsession. Obsessions rivet your attention to yourself. Over time they make you more and more involved with yourself and with the gratification of your urges and desires. But *love* depends entirely on looking outside of yourself. It gives you the ability and the motivation and the commitment to turn your thoughts away from yourself, while all of your instincts and obsessions are screaming to you to do just the opposite. If you can't love, you can't understand how somebody else feels—you're too wrapped up in yourself to be able to share their joy or feel their pain. When you pour yourself into loving someone, you become brand new. You aren't an island unto yourself any longer but a member of the human family. Only when you enter that human family through your love can you come to know the depth of that family's joy and sorrow, it hopes and dreams, its disappointments, its suffering, its love, and its incalculable strength. You have to be able to love in order to experience and truly feel those things."

"Obsessions are rooted in material drives," he continued, "but love is the essence of spirituality. Love is the only thing you have that is more powerful than your obsessions. When love fills your heart, you're free to live your spirituality. If not, you're a slave to your animal instincts. Don't forget that there's no end to how deep and strong love can be–it's infinite, like God is infinite—but to experience that, you have to immerse yourself in it; you have to let love dominate your life or you won't be able to feel even a fraction of what it can do. It takes real courage to surrender yourself to the unknown, I realize that. But once you do, that decision imparts to you the strength of all those who love you because they, in turn, pour their strength and their love back into you."

"The key," he said, "is to let that happen. To be vulnerable enough to accept love and in your weakness, achieve a strength beyond your wildest imagination. When you surrender yourself that way, when you can strip yourself of the materialistic securities that cushion you in this world, you make room for the emergence of the best part of your humanity, which is the spirituality that you have in common with God. And that, by the way, is exactly how you will **find** God; you find him by opening yourself up to his love."

There was a long silence.

"Did you ever teach a kid to ride a bike?" he asked me.

"No, I never have," I said, wondering where that came from.

"Let me tell you a little story that reminds me of your situation with Ruth. When my son was first learning to ride a bike without training wheels, I'd walk along side of him and hold onto the bike, steadying it as he pedalled along. But he was always afraid that I'd lose my grip and that the bike would crash. So he'd pedal once or twice and then slam on the brakes because he was scared that I'd let him fall if he got going too fast. So for weeks we were the laughing stock of the neighborhood doing our routine on the sidewalk—me holding the bike, him slamming on the brakes every ten feet. Finally he decided to trust me. He pedalled once, then twice, then three times; the bike picked up steam, I kept running with him, he pedalled more, he got more balance and speed, and then off he went on his own. I swear to you, in that instant, it was as if he had been reborn. He had achieved a new freedom because he had found the courage to trust me.

"You've got to let yourself be loved. You've got to be

able to trust the other person with a part of yourself—to give them a chance to make you stronger than you could ever be alone." He paused for a moment and said, "You know, that story of my son gets me thinking about my daughter."

"I thought you only had two boys," I said.

"And one girl. Her name was Ruth, too. We lost her when she was seventeen. She left home one day and disappeared, and we didn't find out until two months later that she had been killed in a car accident. We didn't even get to bury her . . . we didn't find out until she had been dead for two weeks . . . they just sent us some of her things. . . ." He began to cry. "You talk about letting go of your Ruth, but believe me, you shouldn't let people go in this life unless you absolutely have to. It's bad enough when they get taken from you. They're all you've got. They're what make it all worthwhile. . . ." Then he straightened up in bed. There was a long silence. "That's enough of that," he finally said. "If you have any sense, you won't let go of Ruth without a good fight. It sounds to me like all the potential's there for a love that doesn't know any limits. Don't throw it away. You'd regret it for the rest of your life."

I didn't know what to say.

After a few minutes in which neither one of us said anything, he asked me, "Have you ever needed anybody?"

"Sure," I answered. "My parents, when I was a kid. Besides that, though, no, I don't think I've ever really needed anybody. I guess I was always kind of proud of that in a way."

"Don't you know that you can't love anybody if you don't need them?"

"That's not true," I said. "There's lots of people I love, but I don't necessarily *need* them."

"You don't really love anybody if you don't need them. To really love somebody, you have to give them enough of yourself that your life would be changed without them. That's part of what the vulnerability of love is all about—

you love someone so much that you can't be the same without them. That sounds risky, doesn't it. But you have to be willing to be vulnerable that way. Otherwise you don't really love them."

"I guess in a way it's *easier* to love people that you really need."

"That's not what I'm saying. There's a big difference between loving someone because you need them and needing someone because you love them. Your need has to come out of your love, not the other way around.

"You're right, then; it *is* a lot of risk," I said. "Making yourself dependent on somebody just because you love them so much."

The moment I said it, I finally realized why I never cried any more. Ruth was right. She had told me that people only cry at funerals when they lose a part of themselves. The only time you lose a part of yourself when someone dies is when you loved them enough to be a part of them. When you love them enough to need them, you can never be the same without them. The reason I never cried was that I never needed anybody enough—or loved anybody enough—for any part of myself to be affected by what would happen to them. Which was very safe, but incredibly cold on my part.

In a weak effort to defend myself, I said to Sonny, "OK, so I'm afraid of the risk of making myself dependent on somebody else. Big deal. Why *should* I take that kind of risk if I don't have to. It's a dog-eat-dog world out there, you know. Life's a matter of survival of the fittest. It just doesn't make any sense to love, and it definitely doesn't make sense to put yourself in a position of needing any more people than you have to."

"You're right," he said, and he smiled. "If we were animals, it would be stupid for us to love. But we aren't animals. That's the whole point. We aren't just here to survive. We're here to love, like no other animal can do. Love is what gives us a chance to do something better than just survive. It's the chance to be a part of one another by pouring our love into each other. Like I told you, it's the chance to make a human family out of ourselves, rather than just a planet full of animals slugging it out to survive. Like in music when lots of individual notes sacrifice their singular identity in being put together to make harmony. Whether it's two or ten or a hundred or a million people, when they pour themselves together in their love they're stronger and more fulfilled than they could ever be alone. It's like the difference between Mozart and chopsticks. Think back on all the greatest moments in your life; all the times when you felt intensely grateful to be alive. If you think about it enough, you'll realize that most of those moments involved either you loving somebody or somebody else loving you. There's no fulfillment in life like what comes out of love. What could bring you closer to the God of love than to pour your heart out in love for all those of his people who, deep down, have the capacity to do the same for you? We need each other to find that kind of love, to achieve that kind of strength. What else is there to live for but to love?"

"Anyway," he continued, "that's what I think God had in mind in making us like himself. The only unforgivable mistake you can make with God is to insist that you are unlovable and not let him love you. If we had to earn God's love, or if he were to treat us as we deserved to be treated, he would have destroyed us all a long time ago. God doesn't want to have anything to do with that. He loves us. Period. He's not making a list of all the good or bad things we did. He just wants to love us and he wants us to love him. And he wants us to love one another. Not an eye for an eye, or a tooth for a tooth. Not 'I'll scratch your back if you scratch mine.' He wants us to love one another unconditionally. It's hard to do sometimes, but it's worth it. It works wonders. In a way," he added, "faith is just like love. If you don't understand it, if you haven't experienced it, if you haven't let yourself be open to it, then you can't do it.

It's just that simple. The evidence is in the experience. When it happens you'll know. And it's just waiting for you to open yourself up and let it happen."

Sonny became very quiet. Something was trying to come alive in me—whether it was me getting ready to try to make some kind of leap of faith, I don't know. Something was pulling at me inside to find this love that he was talking about, or at least to find that part of myself that was spiritual like God was supposed to be. But it was still hard for me to do that, and it was a constant struggle with old doubts and questions about God and love that kept surfacing as I was trying to put together the things that Sonny was trying to help me understand. One thing I was still stuck on was what a terrible place the world could be—on the people of Auschwitz, how any God could let things like that happen.

After a long silence thinking about it, I sort of abruptly asked him, "If God loves us so much, why doesn't he *do* something about some of the miserable things that happen in this world?"

"Do you think I have an answer for that?" he replied.

"I guess it's a pretty impossible question. Everybody in the world asks that question. There isn't any answer is there, Sonny."

"There's no answer." He was quite for a moment. "But can I give you a perspective?" he smiled.

"Sure. I'll settle for a perspective," I said.

"Suppose that you were God. And let's say, just for argument's sake, that *in your heart* you really loved all the people of the whole world. So you give them a world with enough food to feed everybody (if it's spread around right), and plenty of other good things to offer, and you promise to be right beside every one of them through thick and thin, loving them, suffering with them, sharing everything with them, and helping them. And you ask only one thing of them. That they love one another just as you love them. You want them to share the best part of themselves with one another to be one huge family with strength and peace beyond all imagination."

"Now," he continued, "what would you do if they started killing each other or starving each other?"

"If I were God," I answered, "I'd punish the ones who were responsible. In fact, I'd get them before they even had a chance to start anything. Since I'm God, I would know what they were thinking before they did it."

"But then you'd be taking away their free will. Your people would be just like robots. They'd have no freedom to choose to love, or to let higher principles override their animal instincts. If they weren't doing the right thing, they'd be zapped." He stopped to think for a moment. "But even more than that, why would you take away the suffering in the world that people inflict on one another? You love them all, you want them all to be one. You've given them more than what they need to accomplish that. And then they turn around and kill one another right in front of your eyes. It's true, you know, most of the suffering that goes on in this world is a result of what we do to one another. Not that any one of us brings it on our own self, but as a group some of us make it so that others have to suffer. Why should God be the one to have to do something about that?

"He loves each one of us individually, but I believe that *he made us all to be one,* because he gave us the power to love. So he has to *treat* us like a group. So when one of us asks him to help undo what another has done to them, it's no surprise that he turns us down. It's *our* job to take care of one another and he's given us all the capabilities to do that. *He's got to make us understand that.* He helps each one of us in whatever way he can, and he loves each of us more deeply than we can ever know. But after all he's given us, he's not going to undo what we do to one another. That's not his responsibility. To ask him to do that would be an insult to us—an insult to his creation. He gave us the power to help ourselves.

77

"We've got to take care of one another," he continued. "If he does that *for* us by taking away our free will, we won't be like him any more. We'll never understand what it means to love one another or take care of one another. It's just too bad that after all the terrible lessons of history, we still can't get it straight about what it means to take care of one another. That's not God's fault. It must make him sad to see us waste so much of what we've been given, and then beg him to give us more. He must think we're spoiled brats sometimes. What can he do? All he can do is love us like he does, and help each one of us make the best contribution we can to building up the human family that we were made to be a part of."

Thinking of humanity as a collective group, he was right; it would be foolish for that group to ask God to protect themselves from one another. But as individuals, some are really powerless to change the course of what the group is doing to them. What about these innocent victims, the innocent poor? "Doesn't God listen to them?" I asked him.

Sonny was no stranger to the concept of poverty. First of all, he was dying, which in my book made him poor no matter how much wealth he had. But he didn't have much material wealth either. Like the monks, in a way, he was one of those people who was poor by choice. He lived on a teacher's salary with his wife and two kids. He was by far the best teacher and coach that my high school had ever had, but they could never afford to pay him what he was worth— he had dozens of offers over the years to teach at other places for much more money and better teaching conditions. But his life revolved around the city kids that went there (the monks had built the school in what became one of the worst parts of town). Probably half of his salary went back into the school out of his own pocket—everything from football equipment and basketball nets (for the kids he coached), to computer programs for the kids in his science classes. He had us all over to his house for dinner at least two or three times a year. He and his family lived in a humble apartment in a rough section of town near the school, but they kept it up very well; once you were inside, you knew that these were people who took care of the things they had, and who asked for no more (for themselves) than what they needed.

"Of course God listens to the poor," he said. "He makes himself known to them more deeply than to anybody else in the world. They know how much he loves them, and in their suffering and their vulnerability they know him like no one else can. Believe me, he comes to them in their suffering. They don't have so many things to distract them as other people do. The poor see God like nobody else can. In some ways," he mused, "it's not such a bad idea to be poor." He smiled sort of sadly. "But I'm telling you," he continued, "God means business about wanting us to be a group. As much as he loves us, he'll never undo what we do to one another. He loves us all too much to put us down that way. It's sad for those who get trampled—it's really sad. But God takes care of them in a special way. It's too bad that we can't take care of them better—if we did, it would bring us all much closer to the God who loves us."

"So how does he make himself known to them?"

"He made himself known to them for all time by becoming himself a poor man."

He closed his eyes and was quiet for what seemed to be a very long time.

SEVEN

A Poor Man's Proof for the Existence of God

Not by might and not by power, but by my spirit, says the Lord.

—Zechariah 4:6

My power is at its best in weakness. So I shall be very happy to make my weaknesses my special boast so that the power of Christ may stay over me, and that is why I am quite content with my weaknesses, and with insults, hardships, persecutions, and the agonies I go through for Christ's sake. For it is when I am weak that I am strong.

—St. Paul's second letter to the Corinthians 12: 9–10

"He showed you and me and every person in the whole world how much he loves us by becoming himself a human being."

"Jesus." I knew he would get to that sooner or later. I was very up front with him about it. "Sonny, not everybody believes that Jesus was God's son, and even though I was raised Catholic, I have my doubts about all of that, too."

"That's understandable," he said. "But no matter what you think of him, you can't escape the fact that this one man singlehandedly shaped two thousand years of recorded history since his death."

"I agree, but that doesn't mean he was the Son of God."

"Then why would he have *said* he was?"

"What do you mean?" I asked him.

"Why would he have said *himself* that he was the Son of God, if he wasn't really the Son of God?"

"Maybe he just thought that he was God's Son," I said. "He was a great man. Probably at least some kind of a prophet or something."

"So was he lying? Or was he out of his mind? If he wasn't God's Son, he must have been out of his mind or lying. No great wise person is going to go around saying he's the Son of God if he's not. You see, if you don't believe that Jesus was God's Son, then that means he must have either been lying or he was crazy. So how can you think he was a great prophet? There's no in-between: Jesus was either the Son of God (and telling the truth about it) or he was a liar or he was crazy. Given those choices, keep in mind that in only three years of public life, his example changed the world."

I had never thought about it that way before. I decided just to keep my mouth shut and listen to him, because I had a feeling that he had more to say and that it might be worth listening to.

He thought for a minute and then resumed speaking. "Jesus didn't just save the whole world," he said. "He *shocked* the whole world. Everybody expected him to be this magnificent, all-powerful messiah, and he turned out to be a poor carpenter's son who got crucified when he was 33 years old. He was magnificent all right, but to appreciate what he did, you have to put yourself back into his time, into the situation of the Israelite people who were desperate for a savior. What would you be looking for?"

He waited for me to answer his question. "I'd be looking for somebody who was like God, I guess," I told him. "It would depend on what people thought God was like back then."

81

"Exactly. If you read the Old Testament in the Bible you can understand what the Israelite people were thinking about God before Jesus' time. For one thing, they were scared stiff of God, which is understandable. They had an idea of how powerful he was, and they were a desperate people who depended on him for their survival. He was the almighty who had the power to create and destroy, to win their battles or wipe them off the face of the earth. If they upset him too much, they knew they were finished. But in their hearts, they were very devoted to him, and they knew how much he cared for them. So, to make a long story short, they struck a deal with him, which is called the *old covenant*. It was worded from God's point of view—'I will be your God, you will be my people'—and it basically meant that as long as they followed God's rules (the ten commandments, etc.), then God promised his love and protection. This was their security: God would be there as long as they kept up their end of the bargain. And it was just that—a bargain—a contractual agreement between God and his people.

"Unfortunately, they had it all wrong about God—not that anybody should blame them—all they had to go on were the traditional concepts of God that were handed down from generation to generation. But he wasn't interested in contracts or agreements. He *loved* his people. Unconditionally. But it was hard for them to understand what God's love was all about. Their image of him was as a provider, who would 'scratch their back' if they scratched his. They were very much afraid of losing him. In a sense, they wouldn't let him love them unconditionally. They were very uncomfortable about being 'undeserving' of God's love and protection. When they realized that they weren't holding up their end of the bargain (every time they sinned), they got very nervous that God would just say, 'To hell with you people—I'll find some other people to take care of.' So every time they sinned, it reminded them that what they needed was to somehow clean the slate for all time. They needed a redeemer to make up for all the sins ever committed and to earn God's favor and love forever.

"So now the stage is set for this powerful redeemer to come along. They wait and they wait and they wait for their messiah. Little did they know that what they needed wasn't a *conqueror* type of savior; the redemption that they needed was to learn how much God loved them—they just needed to be shown what God's love was all about. If the message of love could get through to them, they would be saved for all eternity by being enlightened in the understanding that God's relationship to them was one of unconditional love. Then the clean slate and the contractual agreements could be thrown out the window. And they would be able to concentrate more on loving God and loving one another than following rules and contracts (some of them were really hateful people who were getting by thinking that they were holy just because they followed all the rules). So what should God do for them? Should he give them what they're looking for—a redeemer, whose work and sacrifice could make up for the sins of all time? Should he somehow clean the imaginary slate so that everybody could feel better about letting him love them? Or should he just make them understand that they've got it all wrong, and show them in ways that they could comprehend just what his love is all about.

"As it turns out, he does all three of those things in a way that was so perfect, and yet so unexpected and unthinkable, that still, 2000 years later, it's hard to believe it could have really happened. God himself became a man to share our limitations, our lives, our suffering, our sorrows; he taught us how to love, and how love was our very likeness to God, and then in the ultimate act of his love for us, laid down his life by allowing himself to be crucified by us, redeeming in that sacrifice the sins of the whole world.

"But once again, put yourself back before his time. There you are with the rest of the God-fearing world, expecting something awesome to come along—a mighty savior, a king of kings. You would expect him to be admired by all mankind. You would expect him to vindicate God's cause among those who had oppressed the Israelites. And somehow his life, his sacrifice, his cause would be ransom for the whole world—his work so great as to redeem every sin ever committed, and to save man from the eternal punishment that he deserved. You would expect him to put into perspective the troubles of a world of millions. You would expect him to chastise evildoers and to be able to save his chosen people with a flip of his hand, because he was sent from almighty God. But the essence of true redemption was not yet understood.

". . . Enter, the carpenter's son," he continued. "This supposedly powerful king turned out to be a poor shepherd. What was spectacular about Jesus was that he was *nothing* like anybody ever expected. And yet he was perfect. He was precisely what they needed." Sonny pulled his Bible off of his nightstand again, opened it up, and started reading to me.

> See, my servant will prosper
> he shall be lifted up, exalted, rise to great heights.
> As the crowds were appalled on seeing him
> —so disfigured did he look
> that he seemed no longer human—
> so will the crowds be astonished at him,
> and kings stand speechless before him;
> for they shall see something never told
> and witness something never heard before:
> "Who could believe what we have heard,
> and to whom has the power of Yahweh been
> revealed?"
> Like a sapling he grew up in front of us,
> Like a root in arid ground.
> Without beauty, without majesty (we saw him),
> no looks to attract our eyes;
> a thing despised and rejected by men,

a man of sorrows and familiar with suffering,
a man to make people screen their faces,
he was despised and we took no account of him.
And yet ours were the sufferings he bore,
ours the sorrows he carried.
But we, we thought of him as someone punished,
struck by God, and brought low.
Yet he was pierced through for our faults,
crushed for our sins.
On him lies a punishment that brings peace,
and through his wounds we are healed.

"Even though a handful of prophets had predicted that the messiah would have to suffer, no one really interpreted the prophesies to mean that the redeemer would be anything like what Jesus turned out to be. In fact, the world put him to death for being who he was and claiming to be God's Son. They obviously had expected something so completely different that even when he came to live among them and *told* them who he was, they *still* couldn't imagine him being their redeemer. But he was exactly what the world needed. You see, the savior of the world had to save the world by making man's capacity to love the most powerful force in the world. He had to show them that their greatest strength could be achieved only when they made themselves most vulnerable. So he committed the ultimate act of vulnerability in allowing himself to be crucified, sacrificing himself for all the people he loved in the world. And *we* crucified him."

"Can you imagine being in that crowd of people that demanded for him to be crucified? Can you imagine what Jesus must have felt like? Not one of his friends or followers stayed with him in the end. He was all alone. I wonder if it ever went through his mind that he had failed. That he would go down in the history books as a pathetic laughingstock. All the hordes of people yelling at him and hating him. But he went through with it to the end.

Sonny reached to his night stand once again and

opened his Bible to a well-marked page. "You know," he said, "just before Jesus died, he told us what he thought the meaning of life was. He was with his apostles and was praying for them to his Father. Listen to what he said:

> I pray not only for these
> but for those also
> who through their words will believe in me.
> *May they all be one*
> Father may they be one in us
> as you are in me and I am in you. . .
> With me in them and you in me,
> *may they be so completely one*
> that the world will realize that it was you who sent me
> and that I have loved them as much as you loved me.

"He wanted us all to be one. To him, our purpose in life was to love one another so much that all of humanity would work to become *one* in mutual love and shared strength. He prayed that each person and each group of people would pour their love and strength into one another to achieve what would amount to be a massive, cohesive, self-supporting entity—call it the brotherhood of man—unified in the love of God. Think about that. In just a few simple words he tried to hand us the meaning of life, which is something that most people spend their whole life searching for. He taught us that the value of a human being lies *not* in what he or she was born with, but exclusively in how much they love. Every human being—*every person in the world*—has the potential to be the greatest or the least, simply because every human being has the ability to choose whether to love (and love limitlessly) or not to love. That's all that matters in this life.

"In the end, the strength of his love moved the whole world, and when he rose from the dead three days later, he showed the world that in love there is immortality—if you die out of love, you live forever—if you make yourself weak for the sake of love, you gain strength beyond imagination. By his example, he demonstrated how love's strength was in its vulnerability and its gentleness and its endurance. For the first time in history, he taught the world that this great paradox of love was the secret of life. That was what the redeemer was all about. There were times when he had no place to lay his head at night. He wept with man. He bore our sickness and endured our suffering.

"And this man, this word made flesh, this Son of God changed the world forever, because he changed the relationship between God and man by the very example of his love. He gave us a *new* covenant to replace the deal that had stood for ages: '*I give you a new commandment*,' he said, '*Love one another as I have loved you*.' That was it. There were no rules or regulations, no deal that you had to do X to get Y. And in his life, Jesus showed us how God really loves us—he redeemed the world by doing away with man's debt to God (he took the debt upon his own shoulders) and showed us how God's love for us was constant and unconditional. His love was not just a thought or a gesture. He *lived* it when he lived with man, walked with man, turned his cheek to those who hit him and spit on him, and opened his arms to be nailed onto a cross. For God to strip himself of his divinity in the first place was like what it would be for you or me to strip ourselves of our humanity to become like dogs and live and die like dogs. This is what God did for you and me because he loved us completely. *He* was the one who taught us how to love. If you want to be strong . . . then be weak—that was his message. The paradox of his shameful life bore the message of the meaning of love.

"So no one at that time could ever really have predicted what Jesus would be like. They didn't understand what God's love was all about. Even if the most brilliant human mind in the world at that time went to work at dreaming up just what the perfect savior of the world should be like, no one would ever have predicted Jesus. Because no one could understand what redemption was all about until after he came along and showed us. So to those who think that Jesus was just a nice story or a hoax that somebody made up a long time ago, I say that nobody could conceivably have ever *made up* such a story. There's plenty of historical evidence that he existed as a man. And nobody devious enough to want to deceive the world about it's savior would have had the spiritual insight to make Jesus what he was: the gentle, loving, pathetically abused man that he was—and claim him to be the savior of the world. He was a laughing stock. He was a man of tremendous sorrow. He was a lamb taken to the slaughterhouse. He never changed the world at first. Only a few followed him to his disgraceful death. Only a handful believed that he was God's Son. Who would have predicted that such an obscure life could be the plan of salvation for all mankind? And this one man, then, changed the course of human history forever.

"In his life, he showed us that it is love that gives us the capacity to span the limits of our humanity to become fully, fully alive. 'I came,' he said, *'that you may have life and have it to the full.'* " He stopped to think. "In him," he continued, "and only in him, do I see the fullness of God." Sonny stopped and looked at me. Then he smiled. "You have to decide for yourself whether this Jesus was God's son. You have to decide whether his way of turning the world around was some kind of man-made story, or if it truly came from God."

"Now," he said, "I've told you everything. I don't know what else I can say or do to help you understand. If you can believe in love—if you can believe that there exists a spiritual side of yourself—then you can believe in God. The evidence for God lies in the experience of his love. The sacrifice of his Son, the God-made-man who would have died that same death just for you or me, is what you've got to go on to know that God lives and to understand how much he loves you.

"This is the point where the leap of faith comes. You

either believe in this God or you don't. You either accept the experience of this Son of God or you don't. It's not like science where you have something tangible to look at. What you have to do is keep your heart open to being moved by God. What remains is for you to allow him to touch you or speak to you as only he can do. Your belief in the existence of God will come only when you experience him yourself. I've told you what to look for. It's up to you to open yourself up to him. He's waiting for you to do that so he can touch you and be close to you. Use your humanity to think about his love and put his Son's life into a human perspective. The more you think about his life and message, you can't help but fall in love with this man, this God. And if you still doubt, keep in mind that to doubt is to say that this is a made-up story. And I tell you that this story is beyond human thinking. It's filled with truth. Before it actually happened it was really unthinkable, unimaginable—it would have been laughed at. . . ."

"When you talk about him," I couldn't help but tell him, "sometimes I feel like I could put out my hand and almost touch him. I've never felt like that before."

"Let *him* touch *you*. Listen and you'll hear his voice. You've got to find him, and when you do, he'll touch you deeper than you could ever know."

I was moved by his words. "Sonny," I said to him, "People like you shouldn't die."

"Everybody has to die. That's part of life. God gave me life and part of life is death. It's time for me to go to God."

I was very surprised to hear him say that. "I thought you were thinking that God had more plans for you."

"He did. But I've got a feeling that maybe he kept me around just long enough to teach you. I've thought about it the past few days. I think he knew I could help you find him—he wants you to find him because he loves you so much. So he got me to help you. And that's what I've done. I'm glad he gave me the chance. I'm glad *you* gave me the chance. And let me tell you . . . it feels good to be in God's hands when you're dying. I feel peaceful inside now that I feel like I've done what he wanted me to do. . . . If you look for him now, I know you'll find him."

"So all this time when you were saying that God would keep you alive until your work was finished. . . ."

"My friend," he said, "I think this was my work. I didn't realize that before, but I realize it now. It's almost finished. You've almost found him. Maybe it'll still take you a while, but you're almost there. Don't give up. I don't think you need me any more to find him, but just the same, I'd love to still be around when you do. Anyway, I've got a feeling that my time is almost up."

"Don't say that, Sonny."

"It's OK. I'm ready to go to God. I'll be happy with him forever. And I'll be with you more than you know." There was a long silence after that, which wasn't the least bit uncomfortable, that gave me some time to think and absorb what this man was trying to tell me.

After about a half an hour of neither one of us saying a word, I broke the silence and asked him, "What do you think is going to happen after you die? Do you think that there's really a heaven and hell?"

"I think heaven and hell are the same place," he answered.

"That's a strange thing to say, Sonny."

"I had a dream one time. I was riding in a car with a buddy of mine from the Navy, and we got in a head-on collision and we both died. So we floated up to heaven and there was nothing there, no angels, no banquets, no pearly gates, no nothing. And all of a sudden, there was Jesus—I was face-to-face with him and he walked up to me and threw his arms around me and I hugged him like there was no tomorrow; I couldn't let go—it was indescribable. In this dream, I was experiencing the *ecstasy* of being with God in his entirety—something I wanted my whole life.

Anyway he led me to a room—an empty room, and we sat down, and the room had windows to the whole world, but that was it—nothing else. And it was just him and me in the empty room, completely at peace, talking." (As he spoke, I remembered what the old monk had told me about God being the only object of his desire.) "I had never felt so happy or so fulfilled in my life. And that was it. My buddy, meanwhile, was outside, mad as hell, looking for the banquet and the angels and the party, but it was nowhere to be found, and he asked Jesus if there was a TV set or anything, and Jesus said no, this was it. And my buddy ran off cursing and screaming, tearing his hair out because he was so bored and frustrated and disappointed that he would be spending eternity just with God, and nothing else.

"So that dream made me think that maybe heaven is just the eternal presence of God. If you live your life seeking God, and grow to love him deeply and make him the object of your heart's desire, then being with God forever is going to be heaven. If you don't learn about him or grow to love him or seek him in this life, then being with him forever won't mean anything to you. And in that case, the prospect of his eternal presence will be disappointing and frustrating and empty—especially if you see others who are completely happy while you are completely miserable. After all, isn't that what hell is *supposed* to be like? Hell doesn't need to be a fiery furnace to be a place of excruciating torment, especially when you're talking about eternity. Anyway, the choice is yours, but you have to make it before you die. To those who have loved God and desired to be with him on earth, God's presence brings eternal fulfillment and happiness. To those who did not, it is eternal boredom and misunderstanding and frustration and sorrow."

Sonny died two weeks later, after hemorrhaging massively into his lungs.

EIGHT

The Experience of God

I am not sure exactly what heaven will be like, but I do
know that when we die and it comes time for God to
judge us, he will NOT ask, "How many goods things
have you done in your life?", rather he will ask, "How
much LOVE did you put into what you did?"

—*Mother Teresa of Calcutta*

For I am certain of this: neither death nor life, no
angel, no prince, nothing that exists, nothing still to
come, not any power, or height or depth, nor any created thing, can ever come between us and the love of
God.

—*Romans 8: 38–39*

I suppose that would be the end of the story if it
weren't for the fact that, even after all that Sonny had done
for me before he died, I still didn't believe in God. He had
opened my eyes to the prospect of my own spirituality by
making me realize that my ability to love was a reflection of
that spirituality. That had allowed me to realistically consider the possibility of a spiritual being like God. And he
had helped me to understand what God ought to be like
and that Jesus Christ might actually have been the Son of
God. But he was right, too, in what he had told me about
proof for God's existence. The proof was in the experience. As I mourned Sonny's death, I inwardly mourned

the absence of that experience in my own life, and now that Sonny was gone, I felt that the chances of it ever happening were slim or none. What I didn't realize was that the experience of God had been with me for years in the person of Ruth—the girl that I half-loved.

Actually she wasn't "religious" at all. We had talked about religion on numerous occasions, but to her, God was nothing more than a fantasy. Like my friend from Israel, she found it inconceivable that any God could allow the kind of suffering that there was in the world without doing anything about it. And yet, even though I didn't know it at the time, there was more of God's *presence* in her love for me than in anything I had ever known. Ironically enough, this never occurred to me until I practically tried to break up with her, which happened about two weeks after Sonny had passed away, one evening when she and I were sitting around after dinner talking about him.

During Sonny's last weeks in the hospital, I would tell Ruth about all the things that he and I talked about. She would listen to what I had to say with a kind of concentration and interest that, in retrospect, really was out of the ordinary. But she never wanted to go with me to meet him; every time I asked her, she always had an excuse why she couldn't go. I thought it was because she felt uncomfortable around somebody who'd try to get her to believe in God. I found out later, however, that that wasn't the case.

She knew how attached I had been to him, and she never minded it that I spent a lot more time with him—especially toward the end—than I did with her. When he died, she was exceptionally aware of how upset I was about losing not only a friend, but someone whom I had depended on to help me find the God I had looked for all my life. Even though she didn't share any of my enthusiasm for finding such a God, she knew how much it meant to me. In a lot of ways, I was a wreck after Sonny died. Ruth stood by me, and took care of me, and went through it all with me, no matter how painful it was to her when I got down or irritated or downright nasty.

Anyway, we were sitting around talking about him on that particular evening after dinner, and very casually she asked me, "John, did Sonny ever tell you anything about his family?"

"I knew his family," I said. "When I was a senior in high school he used to have us over to his house for dinner. His wife was the salt of the earth. They had two boys."

"Oh."

"Oh yeah, and he said he had a daughter, too, now that I think of it. She died when she was seventeen. It really tore Sonny up. He loved her very much." I noticed Ruth starting to cry.

"She didn't die," she said quietly, the tears streaming down her face.

"He told me she did," I said. "Why are you crying?"

"There's something you need to know about me," she answered. "But I don't know how. . . ."

"What? Tell me."

". . . Sonny was my dad."

I was in shock.

"I never realized it was him you were talking about all this time until a few days before he died. You never told me his last name until then." She struggled to continue. "I ran away from home when I was seventeen. I ran away for a lot of reasons, but most of all, I guess, because I fell in love with a college guy named Robert. Mom and Dad barely even let me see him when I was at home, Dad didn't like him from the start . . . so we ran off to a little podunk town in Illinois where Robert had some family. Dad spent all kinds of time and money chasing after me, trying to find me and get me back home, and he tried to go after Robert with the police and lawyers and everything. It was pathetic and embarrassing and humiliating for all of us. So, to make a long story short, Robert thought the best thing for everybody would be if my family thought I was

94

dead. It sounds stupid, and we were stupid, but he talked me into it. He got some of his friends to write letters and call my family and make it all sound official, and he sent them some of my things. They made it sound like I had been killed in a car accident when I was off on my own and my car landed in a river and they never found my body.

"Anyway, my mom and dad believed all of it, and they didn't bother us any more. But about six months after I 'died' Robert turned on me, and started beating me up. He tortured me, John. He did things to me which I don't know if I'll ever be able to talk about them to anyone. He taught me how to hate God because of what he was, and I hated God so much after what he did to me that I don't think I could have ever looked my poor innocent father in the face again because I knew that the only thing he wanted for me in this world was for me to love God. Anyway that went on for almost a year with Robert and then I finally got away from him and came back to the city, but I never had the heart to go back to my parents. I knew that they were struggling trying to raise the boys and that they didn't need me to complicate things—as it was, they were in debt up to their gills from the money they had spent trying to get me home. So I never went back. I've always thought about it, and I've come close so many times, but I'm sure they would have just hated me for it and I don't blame them . . . and now Dad's dead and I never saw him. . . ." She broke down and sobbed uncontrollably.

I didn't know what to say to her, she looked so pitiful. It was hard for me to empathize with her in a way, because the whole thing sounded so crazy. I almost wanted to "slap some sense into her" for being so impulsive and immature in the first place, and then for projecting her own self-hatred onto her parents. What was *wrong* with her, I wondered. Perhaps there was more to the story than what she was telling me. That's the only way I could make any sense out of it.

In retrospect, after the initial moments of shock wore

off, no matter how strange and serendipitous it all was, I'd have to say that it was a fitting turn of events—"fitting" because it suddenly occurred to me that I was face-to-face with a woman, who, in a sense, was living proof of the *failure* of Sonny's message. This was scary to me. I had always (at least up until now) respected Ruth's intellect and judgment tremendously, and for her to have been so heavily exposed to Sonny's ideas and perspectives, and then to not believe in God . . . really put to question the credibility of Sonny's message (at least to me). Being Sonny's daughter, and being in the dire straights she was in, she must have looked for God as thoroughly and as desperately as anyone ever could, but she never found him. When she most desperately needed him he failed her. She had experienced the bitter disappointment of the absence of a God she had been taught to look for all her life. It wasn't so much that Ruth hated God—it was *worse* than that. She just stopped believing in him. Ruth was an atheist. Had she herself, in her pursuit of God, proved that he didn't exist?

This immediately aroused in me a new curiosity about her as if she had already travelled a long and possibly dead-end road that I was just now embarking on. In a way, it made me feel almost a new kind of comradery with her; we were people whom Sonny had taught to find God—"set up" as it were, for the disappointment of a lifetime. I wanted to ask her how it went for her and where she looked for God . . . and most of all how and when she decided to stop looking. I wondered if I would have to spend the rest of my life looking for God to find him, or if indeed it was all just going to be an enormous disappointment—I hoped against hope that it wouldn't, but I couldn't help but wonder. Perhaps in looking carefully but never finding God, Ruth had proved to herself that he didn't exist.

But then, I thought to myself, if she really got the same message from Sonny that I did, how could she ever give up on God? I knew that something inside of me (not *all* of me, but something inside of me) would have looked for him forever, knowing as I did then what he would mean to me. Maybe Ruth gave up too early. Maybe she was so wrapped up inside of herself with other worries that she was unable to see God around her. Or maybe Sonny's message never really got through to her after all—if it had gotten through to her like it had gotten through to me, maybe she would have never given up.

Then, I let myself imagine that perhaps by some chance coincidence, fate had ordained *me* to be responsible for getting Sonny's message through to her, since Sonny wasn't able to do it himself. Perhaps whether he knew it or not, the only way he had of rescuing his daughter was to rescue me. He died with his message on his lips so that someone like me who happened to stumble onto it could carry it on—carry it back even to the daughter he thought was dead, to bring her to life in the experience of God. After all that Sonny had done for me, I thought to myself, this was my chance to help him. How strange are the ways in which our lives are connected.

Just as this thought entered my mind, however, a darker side of myself emerged; a blanket of selfishness and weakness began to obscure my vision of God and smother the humanity in my soul. I started to entertain the idea that this new development in my understanding of Ruth was giving me an unexpected chance to free myself from a lot of difficult problems all at once. It was a golden opportunity not only to break free from my entanglement with Ruth, but also to escape from what might turn out to be a *hopeless* pursuit of God. I had the chance now to justifiably hate Ruth for not being with her father when she knew he was dying. Ruth had finally done something unforgivable to me and to her father and now I could justifiably make her pay for that. I wouldn't have to feel guilty or torn any more about not loving her fully—I was off the hook; I could make a clean break from all the ties, the attachments, the uncertainties, and just get on with my life and never have to look back.

Of course, there was something about this whole way of thinking that immediately struck me as cruel and arrogant on my part. It surprised me (and scared me in a way) to know that I could spin around so fast and cower in the fear of an unwanted commitment. That I could run away from my problems so quickly when given even half a chance—and turn my back on people who loved me. Who was I to cast this stone at Ruth? But then who was Ruth to torment me with her hang-ups and misunderstandings, and the strange distance that kept us in the dark from one another.

I finally realized that this was my moment of truth, not just about Ruth, but about God as well. This was the test of my love and devotion—perhaps of my humanity itself. Would my love be the strength of my life, or would it disintegrate in the face of this challenge. As much as it was an opportunity to get myself off the hook, it was an opportunity, too, to love Ruth all the more for this strange mistake, and in doing so help her dissolve the barriers that separated her from me. If I kept up my pursuit of God and somehow was able to take her to God with me, she would never again have to be afraid or hate herself or hide behind her defenses—she would be able to be her wonderful self and walk with the strength and peace and love of a living God. But could I trust her to come out of her shell in the first place? Could I trust myself and the message of her father that it was worth it to try and find God? Both Ruth and God were testing me now (did they both realize that?) and they were waiting for an answer. Would I play it safe or would I love? Was this more my chance to save Ruth or Ruth's chance to save me?

So now Ruth had forced the two most monumental issues of my life by uttering that simple fact that Sonny was her Dad. This was my moment of truth. I could rid myself of her uncomfortably deep and powerful love and end my pursuit of God (in response to the "lesson" of her own failure to find him) . . . *or* I could bring her closer to me than I had ever imagined, and take her with me to God. There really was no in-between. No longer would I be able to ride the fence—neither with God, nor with love. My life was now inextricably enmeshed in the decisions I had to make in response to those two overwhelming questions. I would have to do something now. I made my decision.

I decided to bail out. I could live *without* Ruth, and probably without God. My weakness prevailed and I breathed an instantaneous, but very short-lived sigh of relief in the face of the woman who ultimately, because of the depth of her love, would save my life and bring me to a God whom she herself did not yet even know.

"I'm really sorry that bastard beat you up and hurt you," I said. "But as far as not going back to your parents is concerned, that's the stupidest thing I ever heard in my life. They *loved* you. Don't you realize that Sonny would have given anything, *anything* to see you again before he died? How could you not go to visit him if you knew he was dying?" I really put it to her.

"I thought I would just make him worse."

"Ruth, the man was *dying*."

"I know, John. I would have gone. But I thought he hated me."

"You're pitiful!" I shouted. "Pitiful!"

"Please don't be mad at me, John," she cried. "I loved him. But I was sure he'd hate me. I hated myself for how stupid I was. . . ."

"So you took it out on him."

"Oh, I don't even know why I told you," she exclaimed, very nervously, watching every expression on my face, "because now you hate me, too."

"You just don't get it, do you, Ruth. You're so wrapped up in hating yourself, you can't think of how anybody else feels."

"I do!" she cried, "I think of *you*. You're all I think of. I don't care about myself. All I care about is you."

"That's a lie. If you didn't care about yourself you

99

wouldn't be so careful about what you say and what you've kept from me. You *can't* care about me. Because you can't love me. You don't know *how* to love me. And I don't know how I could ever love you."

At that instant I really did want to walk away from her forever, but the minute I said it, I regretted it. It was a stupid thing for me to say. I was more to blame than she was for her not being able to love me. I was the one who always pushed her away and I shouldn't have been surprised that that made her feel bad about herself. I knew that she loved me more than anybody in the world loved me, and I loved her too. But I was angry as hell, and that's what came out.

Unfortunately, I might as well have taken a baseball bat and smashed her in the head with it, because that was the effect it had on her. It was too much for her to take. She suddenly became very quiet and cried for a little while, and then she softly just told me to go away, and never to come back again. Oddly enough, the moment that she let go was the moment when I really fell hopelessly in love with her—it was at that moment that my "toothache" lifted, and I could see her for what she really was. And she was beautiful. She had been hard for me to love because she had always *tried* so hard, and she had been hard to talk to because she was constantly on guard—trying to hide from me the things she thought were bad about herself. But most of that was because of what I had been doing to her, without really knowing what I was doing. Immediately I wanted her back. I tried to explain to her what was happening in me, but at that point she was much too hurt to let me near her. She wouldn't listen to a word from me, and I had no choice but to go away and leave her alone.

I later found out that aside from failing to love Ruth, I had misjudged her very badly. I didn't know it at the time, but there was more to the story of her leaving home than falling in love with a crazy college kid. I didn't find this out until the next day, but I think it's best to mention at this point what the rest of the truth *was*. The real reason why she ran away with Robert was that she had been raped at home by one of her uncles, and there was no way to protect herself from him in her parents' house. He would come over to the house to help "babysit" the younger kids in the family; for a period of months he made subtle advances to try to have his way with Ruth, and finally one time he did. She was young and very scared and he warned her not to ever tell her parents. He threatened her that if she did, he would tell her parents that she "liked it" and that she wanted him to do it—basically that she had seduced him. So she kept quiet and faced it all alone. It obviously made her feel very cheap and terrible, and she resented her mom and dad for being too naive to know what her uncle had been doing to her. She just wanted to get out of the house and be with Robert because Robert made her feel good, and she needed to feel good. She has since told me many times about the recurrent nightmares she has had of her uncle tearing off her nightgown and smashing her face against his chest, smothering her so she couldn't scream, violating her without even looking at her.

Again, I didn't know any of this at the time, and I didn't find out any of it until the next day. Not that it gives me any kind of excuse for wanting to run away from her or for saying the things I said to her that day, but I just had no idea. Even in her anxiety over the prospect of losing me, she hadn't been able to bring herself just yet to tell me what had really happened to her, to explain the secrets of her running away and the curious distance she kept between herself and all of the people that she wanted to love.

Anyway, I went home that night wondering what I was going to do, and I stayed awake all night thinking about it. If there was any God around, now was when I needed him, I thought, to get me out of the mess I had made for myself. The phone rang at 4 in the morning and it was the hospital calling. Ruth was in the intensive care unit, having tried to kill herself with a bottle of aspirin. Mine was the only phone number in her pocketbook when they found her. So much for God, I thought to myself.

I rushed off to the hospital, and I was starting to wonder now if my own life was worth living, after all of the pain I had caused her. She had suffered enough in her life, and now I had heaped more on top of her because I was mad and because my feelings were a little hurt. By the time I got there, she was just waking up from being unconscious; she was doing much better than when they had first called me. She was a little groggy but sitting up in bed, and as soon as she saw me she became very alert, but continued to stare straight ahead and not look at me. As I watched her the corners of her lips quivered and the quivering became more pronounced and erratic as she strained her face to stop herself from crying. As I approached her bedside she continued to stare straight ahead and started mumbling something. Her hair was completely dishevelled, her face looked wrinkled and washed out all over and she was sitting up sort of slumped over with her head up. She was pathetic. It hurt me to look at her, but I was completely in love with her, more at that moment than I had ever been.

To see her and to hear what she was mumbling would have broken anyone's heart. Every time I think of it something inside of me wants to curl up and die. By the time I figured out what it was that she was saying, she had started softly, limply slapping herself in the face, saying, "Bad me, what a bad me," as if she were scolding a small child. "You don't deserve to live, you can't do anything right . . . bad me, bad, bad me . . ." and intermittently she would just groan or burst out in tears for a little while. I stood by her bedside and held her hand and just watched for a few minutes, so completely at a loss was I for anything appropriate to say. I would have done anything to stop her from feeling like that and saying those things. Nothing I could think of, however, would have sounded right or made the slightest difference to this suffering woman whom I now loved so much. I wasn't even sure if she would hear what I was saying because she continued the whole time to stare straight ahead, slapping her face, and resisted all of my efforts to gain eye contact with her.

"Ruth," I said finally, "you can't do this to yourself. You're going to be OK."

"What do you mean I'm going to be OK," she softly moaned through her tears. "I'm not OK. You know I'm no good. You don't understand anyway. You could never understand." She started to cry a little harder, and there was such obvious pain in her face that it was almost impossible to look at her for more than a moment at a time without literally becoming sick to my stomach to see her like that. I tried and tried to talk her down or comfort her, but she would have no part of it. She continued to say the same things over and over again, never really answering what I asked her, never following any line of reason—she was just completely absorbed in her own self-disgust. Anything I said to compliment her or try and make her feel better about herself, was answered with a simple shake of her head, "no", or on occasion a sad, weak smile that said, "I know you're just saying this to get me to stop crying, its not really true and I know it."

She was absolutely impenetrable, a model of perfectly executed self-destruction for whom I could do nothing, except to watch her consume herself and fall more and more deeply into what seemed to be an irretrievable state of self-hatred. I never knew that she was *capable* of hating herself so much, and yet I never had been able to know her well enough to know that it was possible. Indeed, the world and I had been very hard on her. In loving me she had tried to overcome the pain and insecurity and self-hatred that her past had imposed. But now that I was gone, everything came down on her at once. And this was the result. As I watched this happening before my eyes, I thought about what my relationship to this human being had been, and what I should have to do with someone so severely damaged by the world and by what I myself had done to her. And there was suddenly a sense of hopelessness in me because here was one person to whom I wanted to give my love and promise my devotion, and she was destroying herself and there was nothing I could do to stop her from it. For the first time in my life I felt the utter destitution of anticipating the loss of someone whom I needed, someone whom I was not sure that I could live without.

And so for the first time since I was a small boy, as I sat on the bed with Ruth and held her hand, I began to cry. At first I cried softly, but then the urge to cry got stronger—as that urge got stronger, my despair deepened, and the crying became uncontrollable. There was one thing about it that was almost comforting about crying: the harder I cried the closer I felt to Ruth, the better it felt to cry. Whatever the case was, I could not stop crying; at that point I don't think I wanted to stop. What was amazing, was what happened to Ruth when she saw me crying. She immediately stopped staring, she looked into my eyes, and it was obvious that in that fleeting moment she had changed completely. I guess something had happened to her in seeing me crying so desperately over losing her and seeing her in so much pain that made her realize, for the first time, just how much she meant to me. It was as if in an instant she completely forgot about herself, and turned all of her attention to me. She put her arms around me and gently pulled my head to her breast and cried with me and begged me—BEGGED me— to stop crying, that she couldn't stand to hear me cry, that everything would be OK and she would do anything if I would just stop crying. She explained to me the rest of the truth about her past, and why she had felt the way she did, and that she was sorry she had been so wrong to think that everyone would hate her for what she did.

Through my tears I tried to mumble what I felt to her, that I needed her, and look what I had done to her, and now she wanted to take her own life away, and now I felt almost like taking my own life away because I couldn't go on without her. And you should have heard her, she held me all the tighter and tried to quiet me down and told me never to say that again about taking my own life away, and that she would never leave me. And that's when it happened. For the first time in my life, I felt the presence of God. He touched me in Ruth's tears, he whispered in Ruth's voice. He had shattered, finally *shattered* the walls that had kept me from seeing him, the same walls I had built up to keep from being hurt and to keep from needing or really loving anyone else—the same walls that had kept me from crying all those years. And now I was crying and I knew I was loved more intensely than I ever had been before, and at that moment he touched me. And from that moment on nothing was the same. Nothing would ever be the same again.

This was how I came to know God. After all the years of doubt and indecision, I now knew for sure that God existed, like trees and rocks and my body existed. From that point on, he was *visible* to me in a way I had never even understood before, and since then, not a day has gone by without at least one moment of my experiencing God's presence in the things that happen in the world around me. Some days are filled with the sensation of his touching me or whispering to me or holding me. There are days, too, when I feel alone, but even in the depth of times of desperation I know deep inside me that he is there. He's with me constantly. He's with us all constantly. No argument or disappointment or theory could ever take him away from me, so strong was this proof for the existence of God.

NINE

The Requirement

"Lord, when did we see you hungry or thirsty, a
stranger or naked, sick or in prison, and did not come
to your help?" Then he will answer, "I tell you sol-
emnly, in so far as you neglected to do this for these
least of my brothers, you neglected to do it for me."
— *Matthew 25: 45–36*

This above all: to thine own self be true
And it must follow, as the night the day,
Thou canst not then be false to any man.
— *HAMLET, Act I Scene III,* William Shakespeare

Ruth recovered quickly, and the first thing she did
after she left the hospital was to go back to her family and
tell her mother how sorry she was about what had happened. She was bitterly sorry about Sonny, and she explained to her mother the truth about why she left home,
and what a terrible mistake she had made, and that all she
wanted was to reconcile herself with her family and not
waste any more time apart. Ruth's mom was more than
receptive to her. She took her in her arms and blamed
herself for the terrible circumstances that caused Ruth to
run away. When Ruth asked her how she was able to manage with Sonny being gone, they both broke down and
cried. After a while her mom said, "You know Ruth, your
Dad always belonged to God. He was never really mine,

but he had a wonderful way of making me feel OK with that. Someday I know I'll be with him." That was all she could manage to say without breaking into tears again.

Ruth and I got married six months later. That, too, might be a good place to end this story, except for something that happened to us just before our wedding that I think was almost as important as everything else combined. The priest that we asked to marry us was the old monk (his name was Father Austin) who had told me the thing about being sent to his room to find God. He wanted to meet with us a few times before our wedding so that he could get to know us better, and one night we decided to take him out to dinner to a nice Italian restaurant. Toward the end of the meal, he asked us why we wanted to get married in the church. So Ruth and I told him how we had come to know God, and how our faith was the most important thing in either one of our lives, and that we wanted God to be at the center of our marriage, just like we wanted him to be at the center of everything else we ever did.

The old monk just looked at us quietly and smiled. After about a minute of silence he looked over at Ruth then looked at me and said, "What is it that you're going to *do* with that faith of yours that you think God is going to be at the center of all of it?"

"We're going to get married and we'll spend the rest of our life with God in whatever we do," I said.

"What *are* you going to do?" he asked patiently.

"I don't know, father. Why?"

"If your faith is real, it should be telling you what to do," he said.

"I don't think it has yet."

"Do you remember the story in the Bible about Cain and Abel?"

"Sure, but I thought somebody made all that up." I just assumed that he was changing the subject.

"Probably."

"I forget who killed who."

107

"Cain killed Abel," he replied. "Do you remember what Cain said to God after he killed Abel, when God asked him where his brother was?"

"I do remember that part," I said. "He was real smug about it. He looked up to God and said, '*Am I my brother's keeper?*'"

"Am I my brother's keeper. . . ." he reiterated slowly. Then he looked straight at me. "You know," he said, "Cain never got an answer to his question. God has waited for us to come up with an answer to that question for the last four thousand years. Each man has to come up with his own answer." Then he was quiet for a moment. It was near the end of the meal, and I was sort of hoping I could get the check before the conversation got too much deeper. "Are you," he asked me, "your brother's keeper?"

"I guess it depends," I answered, "on who I define as my brother."

"Exactly."

"What does that have to do with faith?" I asked.

"Your faith should tell you who your brothers are."

I thought about it for a moment. "We're all sons and daughters of God," I said. "He loves us all the same. He made us all to be one by loving one another as he loves us. So I guess all men and women are my brothers and sisters."

"So are you, or are you not your brother's keeper?"

"I want to be," I said.

"So what are you going to do about it?"

"I don't know. What can I do?"

"You can help out the ones who are in trouble," he said, "who haven't been as lucky as you have. You can give them your time and your work and your heart. You can help them find God. You can pray constantly for them so that God will help them more. God listens to prayers, you know. Prayer is a powerful thing when you consider what you've got on the listening end. And there's another thing you can do. You can take some of the material 'extras' that

108

you have—things that you don't need—and give them away to your brothers who are in dire need."

"Like what?" I asked him.

"Whatever you can do without," he replied. That was all he said. The check came, and even though I knew it was going to be expensive, the total was even more than what I had anticipated. As I looked over the items on the bill, I noticed out of the corner of my eye that the monk had picked up a large piece of a roll that had been on his plate and was wrapping it in a clean handkerchief that he had pulled out of his pocket. I glanced over at Ruth and she, too, was watching him out of the corner of her eye, as she was looking for something in her pocketbook. Then the monk quietly stuffed the wrapped roll into the side pocket of his coat.

I didn't know whether to say anything or not, but my curiosity got the best of me so I awkwardly asked him, "Are you still hungry, Father?" Ruth groaned at my lack of manners.

"No, No," he smiled. "I've had plenty. I just didn't want to let anything go to waste."

We left the restaurant and drove Father Austin back to the monastery, wished him good night, and then headed for Ruth's apartment, which was about an hour away. It was late and she was very quiet for the first half of the ride home, but I got the feeling that it wasn't because she was just tired.

"You saw him wrap up that roll, didn't you," I said to her.

"John, we shouldn't go to restaurants like that and spend that kind of money." she replied in a way that made me think she had been waiting for the chance to say it. "It's not right."

"What do you mean?" I asked her. "It's not like we do that every day."

"That roll he wrapped up," Ruth said, "—that roll

could have been a whole meal for a starving kid some-where. We go out and spend a hundred and fifty dollars just for one night out to dinner, and there are hundreds of thousands of people starving to death. I know Father Austin was thinking about that the whole time—the man used to run a mission in South America. I mean he was very polite about it, but you could tell by the look on his face that he was thinking about that."

"It didn't seem to ruin his appetite," I said sarcastically, which I knew I shouldn't have.

"C'mon, John, I know you felt it, too—talking about how all of the people in the world are our brothers and sisters. They don't deserve a meal any less than we do. They don't deserve to die any more than we do. God loves them just as much as he loves us. But we were lucky enough to be born here where we prosper and eat, while the other half of the people in the world die of measles because nobody gives them a 60 cent vaccination, or if measles or malaria or God knows whatever other preventable disease doesn't kill them, they starve to death. It's not fair, John. It isn't."

"You're right. So what can we do?"

"There's no reason why we shouldn't be taking whatever extra money we have and giving them a chance to *survive*, for God's sake—instead of eating out at fine restaurants. Father Austin was right, you know. If you believe in God, you know that those people are our brothers and sisters. Would you let your brother starve to death on your doorstep? Could you face him if he was lying right in front of you and you didn't bother to help him?"

"Of course not. But those starving people aren't exactly at my doorstep," I said.

"Would you listen to yourself? What difference does that make? You know that right now, somewhere in the world, God is with somebody whose dying of starvation just as much as he's with us right now in this car. I think it's a slap in his face to tell him we don't care about the part of him that's inside that poor dying person a thousand miles away. Just because they're far away doesn't mean we should turn our back on them. It's certainly not like we're cut off from helping them. There's such a thing as mail, you know, and boats and trains that carry supplies and things. And even if that was a problem, that they were too far away or that it was too difficult to help them, what about all the poor homeless people that are literally on our own doorsteps. They don't qualify as brothers or sisters?"

"You're right, except for one thing," I said. "People like restaurant workers have to earn a living, too. If people like us didn't eat out at restaurants, then all of the people who work in the kitchen or wait on tables would be out of a job. Then maybe they'd be on the streets, so indirectly that's helping to keep them from starving or being homeless."

"You're rationalizing. And I'm going to rationalize right back at you." She took a moment to think. "I agree with you that putting money into restaurants creates jobs for restaurant workers. But putting money into world missions creates jobs for mission workers—and on top of that, the work that is done is to help people who are dying, rather than providing a luxury to people who want to have a nice dinner. Whoever pays the money picks the cause. Wouldn't it be better to put our money into a cause that's going to keep somebody from starving to death? It's totally within our control (and our ability) to do that. And sometimes I think that since we have the *power* to easily save that dying brother of ours . . . if we just decide to turn our back on him and let him die . . . we might as well be killing him. What's the difference?"

"You're making me feel so guilty I can't stand it," I said.

"I'm not trying to *make* you feel guilty. We both feel guilty because we know that those are our brothers and sisters. I just think we never really thought about it before. Now we have to decide what we're going to do with what we know."

111

"I guess that's the end of the hundred dollar dinners—I can see that right now," I said. "But I'm wondering how far does it have to go? How much *can* we spend on dinner without having to feel bad about it? How much should we spend on other things? Do we give up everything we have and give it away to the poor? I don't know."

"I don't know either. But whatever we do, it shouldn't be out of guilt. We're not doing it for ourselves, we're doing it for people who we can love like God loves us. I'm not necessarily saying that we should *never* go out to dinner. Just that we should think more about what we're doing. And try to love somebody else out there who we may not even know, but who's just as much a part of God as we are. He or she is out there working just as hard as we do (just to *survive*); he or she has a family just like we do, has hopes and dreams and disappointments just like we do; feels pain and warmth and love just like we do. Why can't we try to love them?"

"We can, Ruth. We can." It was a lot to think about. For most of my life, I had taken for granted the many material things that I was so lucky to have. I always *knew* that more than half of the people in the world went to bed hungry every night, but I just didn't think about it that much. In taking my priveleged status for granted, how could I have forgotten about all of my brothers and sisters? Was I assuming that I was somehow better or more deserving of a comfortable life than the millions of people in the world who were struggling to survive? Whatever it was, I made up my mind that I wasn't going to do it any more, but at the same time I knew it would be hard for me to ever part with some of the material advantages I had in life, which I had gotten used to. Just how far would I be willing to go to help the desperate cause of my needy brothers?

About a week later, we went to see Father Austin again, and told him about what we had talked about on the ride home from taking him out to dinner. I told him, too, about what I was struggling with in terms of the practical question of "how far to go" in giving what I could to the poor. If I wanted to, I could end up nearly broke with just enough to get by on. Is that what God would want?

When I asked the monk that question, he told me exactly what Ruth had already said: not to do anything out of guilt, but out of love. "Try to take for yourself only what you need," he said. "We're not talking about starving yourself, or denying yourself or your children a safe place to live or a good education. God wants us to have a good life and enjoy the beauty of this creation. Just try not to take for yourself any more than you need."

"But how do you decide what you need and what you don't need?" I asked him.

"That's something only you can decide. Some people get by on very little, and still find fulfillment and happiness beyond imagination. If God is what you want in this life, your faith will tell you what you need." At that, he picked up a Bible that was sitting on a coffee table in the room where we were sitting and thumbed through it quickly. When he found the passage he was looking for, he read it to me.

"He was setting out on a journey when a man ran up, knelt before him and put this question to him, "Good master, what must I do to inherit eternal life?" Jesus said to him,". . . . You know the commandments: *You must not kill; You must not commit adultery; You must not steal; You must not bring false witness; You must not defraud; Honor your father and mother.*" And he said to him, "Master, I have kept all these from my earliest days." Jesus looked steadily at him and loved him, and he said, "There is one thing you lack. Go and sell everything you own and give the money to the poor, and you will have treasure in heaven; then come, *follow me*. But his face fell at these words and he went away sad, for he was a man of great wealth."

Then the old monk closed the book.

"The story never says whether or not he gave his money away," I said to him. Ruth kicked me.

"That's exactly right," he replied. "Every man in his own heart has to make his own decision about whether or not to give away what he can. If you were the rich man, what do you think you would have done?"

"I suppose I'd give it all away, if Jesus was standing right there asking me to, but it would be hard to do."

"Very hard, indeed. But let me tell you something. Jesus *is* standing right here. If you have faith, you have to believe that. He's with you every moment. And all he asks is that you love your brothers just as he loves you. Sometimes that means taking care of them when they don't have enough to eat, that's all. You have to listen to him. You have to believe in him as if he were standing in front of you in the flesh. If you have faith, you know he's with you."

"He asked a lot of the rich man," I remarked.

"He asks a lot of us all. But what he asks for is nothing in comparison to what he gives. Really." He stopped for a moment and smiled, then continued. "I read you that passage because I want you to think. I'm not telling you to sell everything you have. Just be careful about deciding what you need and what you don't need, because there is a world of people to love out there who are in desperate need. And the temptation in this busy society of ours is to not think about them, especially when they're off somewhere in another country, and to not realize when we have an opportunity to do something that might even mean the difference between life and death for them. We *can* help them, at least a little bit. And let's face it, if we *can* help them, but we make the decision *not* to—either by not thinking about it or just flat out refusing to do *anything* about them—we might as well be handing them their death sentence. And if that's the case, we might as well forget all about believing in God; anybody who can let that happen and choose to turn away from it or not think about it has no idea who God is. No idea." He paused for a moment,

114

then said, "Rich people criticize poor people all the time when they steal out of desperation or fight one another for material possessions. If you want to help a poor man see God, share what you have with him. Help him to see in you that material things are meaningless when God is your life. Make yourself poor and inherit the fullness of the spirit of God."

"Father, not everybody has money to give."

"Of course not. But it's not just money that the world needs. Do you have some time to give somebody you know who's lonely? Do you have a skill you can teach somebody? Can you let somebody know that you care about them when nobody else seems to? Can you pray? It all comes down to this: we're all one family. God loves every last one of us more than he loves himself. If we don't share our lives with one another, pour our love into one another, and draw our strength from one another, we don't live. All we have to do is let the God of love fill our hearts. His love is strong and it's real. So chase the other things out and let God fill your heart. Let your love be your guide. Let love be your life."

Ruth and I were married one month later, and have prayed every day of our married life that nothing will ever get in the way of us letting love be our life. Sonny's proof—our proof for the existence of God, a proof that we found in each other—has kept our faith strong even when we, as people, are most weak. There are dark days in our lives when our vision of God is obscured and our faith is tested, but part of what it means for us to love God and for him to love us and for us to love each other is that we get through those times. Part of love is reaching through the unknown, and sometimes we grow stronger in dealing with things we cannot fully understand. The world has tried many times to fool us into thinking that there is no more to life than what our senses can perceive. But thanks to God and Sonny Joseph, we know better.

About the Author

John N. Constantino M.D., is a resident physician at the Bronx Municipal Hospital Center in New York. His long-standing interest in theology began in religion courses taught by Benedictine Monks of the Saint Louis Priory, and continued in his studies of philosophy at Cornell University, where he graduated with distinction in 1984. He began writing *A Poor Man's Proof for the Existence of God* while at the Washington University School of Medicine in St. Louis. As a student there, he cared for a patient dying of lung cancer, whose extraordinary faith in God inspired the creation of the main character of this story. Dr. Constantino and his wife and daughter live in the Bronx, New York.